Preaching the Calendar

PREACHING THE CALENDAR

Celebrating Holidays
and Holy Days

J. Ellsworth Kalas

Westminster John Knox Press
LOUISVILLE • LONDON

Scripture quotations, unless otherwise indicated, are from the New Revised Standard Version of the Bible, copyright © 1989 by the Division of Christian Education of the National Council of the Churches of Christ in the U.S.A., and used by permission.

Book design by Sharon Adams
Cover design by Eric Walljasper, Minneapolis, MN

First edition
Published by Westminster John Knox Press
Louisville, Kentucky

This book is printed on acid-free paper that meets the American National Standards Institute Z39.48 standard. ⊚

PRINTED IN THE UNITED STATES OF AMERICA

04 05 06 07 08 09 10 11 12 13—10 9 8 7 6 5 4 3 2 1

Library of Congress Cataloging-in-Publication Data
Kalas, J. Ellsworth, 1923–
    Preaching the calendar : celebrating holidays and holy
    days / J. Ellsworth Kalas.
        p. cm.
    Includes bibliographical references.
    ISBN 0-664-22714-7 (alk. paper)
    1. Sermons, American—20th century. I. Title.

    BV4253.K35 2003
    252'.6—dc22   2003066552

Contents

Introduction:
The Preacher and the Calendar

Biblical faith has always had a primary stake in the calendar. A historian would no doubt challenge any suggestion that the Bible invented the calendar, but the idea is implicit in the book of Genesis. The creation story unfolds on a structure of days, "morning and evening," then counts out seven to give us a week. There's something so wonderfully simple about it; some would even say, simplistic.

Anthropologists would argue for something earlier in our human experience, something more mystical, if not religious. They ponder the human inclination to look at the moon as it diminishes, then grows again, and from that observation establish a schedule of the several phases of the moon. Some have suggested that our earliest ancestors watched as days grew shorter and contemplated that the world might be coming to an end. It could be so, because one can speculate almost anything about our ancestors and know that probably someone once felt that way. But such an explanation for our human experience seems more rooted in the poetic than in the scientific.

And for that matter, Genesis is probably closer to a poet's vision than to a scientist's. When it majestically unfolds the creation story, it makes the event accessible to any human being by giving it a framework of mornings and evenings. We humans live by just such mornings and evenings, and we're comfortable with a creator who works with the same sort of timetable.

But more than that, we humans are creatures with an instinctive feeling for time. Perhaps it's our sense of mortality that makes us so. Humans who carry a timepiece with them are very new on the human scene; indeed, even those who had a sundial or its equivalent go back only a few centuries. But a sense of time is at the essence of who we are. The writer of Genesis is not many lines into the story without a tacit acknowledgment of that fact.

After the Jews began to be a nation, the calendar gained dramatic new significance. Days were not simply elements of nature; now they were sacred history. Other nations might mark off seasons for their importance in the planting and harvesting of crops, and of course the Jews would do the same. But they went far beyond that. When God instructed Moses and Aaron about their exodus from Egypt, it was with the word "This month shall mark for you the beginning of months; it shall be the first month of the year for you" (Exodus 12:2). The Jews were not to be satisfied with a calendar that offered a collection of holy days; the calendar would itself be a declaration of their faith.

Specifics would develop from there. There would be the Sabbath, which would come to seem the very reason for the week's existence and the identifying mark of the Jew even beyond circumcision. They would have holy days and occasions, too, ranging all the way from Passover and the Day of Atonement to the Year of Jubilee. But all these would be *faith* days, linked to their walk with God and generally celebrating some instance of God's care for them as a people.

It isn't surprising, then, that we Christians are also a calendar people. In some cases, we have appropriated the Jewish events, with the Sabbath becoming Sunday; the Passover, Holy Communion; and Pentecost, the celebration of the coming of the Holy Spirit. But we also have Advent and Lent, Christmas and Easter, Ash Wednesday, Maundy Thursday, and Good Friday. Students of world religions say that we Christians have sometimes co-opted pagan days to our own purposes. If so, they've tended to be happy conversions, at least from our point of view.

But it is surprising that we haven't done a better job, especially in typical Protestantism, in *preaching* the calendar. In fact, some preachers dread these special days because of the difficulty in preaching them well or because they fear being repetitive. Many pastors approach Christmas and Easter with particular uneasiness. They know they will be greeted by more believers and potential believers than at any other time, but they aren't sure how to speak a word that is old enough to warm the heart and new enough to engage the mind. And as for the days of the secular calendar—New Year's Day, Valentine's Day, Martin Luther King Jr. Day, Independence Day, to name a few—we're inclined to let them remain secular. It seems rarely to occur to us that we might redeem these days and make them assets to our preaching and to the daily faith of our people.

USE THE CALENDAR

The basic message of this book is that we should take full advantage of the calendar. It is a major ally if we will accept it. And it's not presumptuous of us to do so. The editors of *The Oxford Book of Days* remind us that it is "a result of Christianity" that the "calendar of ancient Rome has become the modern international standard."[1] They note further that "some holidays that now seem quite secular are based on the Christian calendar." I'm also struck by the fact that many holidays that were never intended to be specifically Christian nevertheless have their roots in the faith commitments of a particular person (as in the case of Mother's Day and Father's Day), or sometimes in the cooperative efforts of religious and secular leaders (Martin Luther King Jr. Day). When we preach the calendar, it isn't an act of usurpation. To the contrary, when we fail to do so, we're losing still another area of life by default.

Over the years, a variety of effective preachers have insisted that we must preach with the Bible in one hand and a daily newspaper in the other. When the holiday is secular, that metaphor applies; but when the day or season is sacred, we have the Bible in both hands while the surrounding culture enviously seeks to stake its claim.

But in these matters the children of this world tend to be wiser than the children of light. When the late Cecil B. De Mille was asked why he made so many biblical spectaculars, he answered to the effect that he wasn't about to lose three thousand years of publicity. The merchant finds a sales motif for every imaginable holiday, sometimes to the point of absurdity. I wouldn't recommend such extremes, but I submit that when newspapers, television, and the Internet are turning the light on a particular day or event, we shouldn't choose to hide in some dark corner of disinterest.

As a matter of fact, the calendar may well be an evangelistic tool. An impressive minority of persons come to church on the first Sunday of the new year with the intention of doing better by God in the year just ahead. The pastor who fails to fold that fact into the sermon or liturgy in significant ways is insensitive to human longing. The superpatriot seeks out church on the Sunday near Independence Day; instead of being chastised for addiction to civil religion, he or she should be embraced by the sermon's attention to civic and civil responsibility. We clergy joke about the Sunday after Easter being "Low Sunday" and observe that the name is appropriate to the attendance. In my own experience as a pastor, I discovered that attendance that Sunday is generally low only by comparison with Easter; in fact, it tends to be above the general average. Why? Because some who put forth special effort to come on Easter find themselves stirred to try again. The effort is noble, even if feeble, and the sermon should be attentive to its possibilities.

True, there's now and then a Scrooge who wants no more reference to Christmas, or whatever other day is special at that moment. But the pastor had better not be Scrooge. Instead, the pastor should be naively hopeful about anything that may make some human soul more open to God and godliness. Preachers sometimes have a mildly cynical streak that causes them to write off some attitudes as "sentimental," "naive," or "unduly patriotic." Such judgments may be correct, but it's also possible that these attitudes are the stable doors by which the

King may enter. If it is true that all poetry begins with a catch in the throat, then one should have respect for every catch in the throat, not knowing what may come from it. It is the preacher's job not to disparage presumably mediocre feelings but to see where there is some possibility in them of elevation.

THE LECTIONARY AND SPECIAL DAYS

But how does the lectionary preacher relate to these special days? When it's a matter of the sacred days that are already part of the lectionary calendar, the preacher simply takes the lectionary still more seriously. In truth, for those of us who grew up without the lectionary (as did the majority of Protestant clergy in America until relatively recently), the emphasis on the lectionary has added wonderful new possibilities to the calendar. A great many preachers in some free traditions still operate with a calendar that rarely gets beyond Christmas and Easter. Blessed is the day when a pastor discovers Pentecost, Ascension Day, and Trinity Sunday.

But ironically, many lectionary preachers fail to take advantage of these days. They use the proper lessons, but they don't necessarily relate the lesson to the day it is intended to celebrate. Many a worshiper leaves such a service having no knowledge, beyond the line in the order of worship that noted "Trinity Sunday," of what the theme of the day means. The sermon managed to keep it a secret. Granted, the Trinity is not the easiest of sermon subjects; but isn't it part of the purpose of the lectionary to lead us into areas we might otherwise overlook or avoid?

So let the nonlectionary preacher enter into the wonder of sacred days heretofore unknown, and let the lectionary preacher take more seriously the potential of this structure. Let the lectionary preacher be saturated in the lessons of the day until he or she finds the logic (sometimes obscure) behind the choice of this lesson for this particular day. And if the logic is obscure, this may only open whole new possibilities of imagination and creativity. But by all means, read the pericope through the lens of the day, if it is in fact a special day. Thus, for instance, one reads Matthew 28:16–20 not simply as a portion from that Gospel but as a strategic insight into a holy day—and in this instance, as a key doctrine of the church. And as surely as having the lectionary has compelled you to eliminate from consideration all other Scripture but the lessons of the day, just so the particular day now compels you to eliminate all other ideas that might occur to you as related to this Scripture. It might, on another day, have to do with missions, or with the sacrament of baptism, or with the ministry of teaching. But not today. If those themes enter your sermon today, they will come in through the overarching theme of Trinity Sunday.

But what shall the lectionary preacher do with secular days, with Mother's Day and such? The purist will recommend giving them simply a tip of the clerical hat, by way of some offhand reference during the course of the sermon or by acknowledging the day during parish announcements and informal moments. That may satisfy the purist, but it doesn't do much for the worshiper who isn't quite that pure (a substantial majority), nor does it help relate the worship of God to the enterprise of common life. The preacher's goal always is to take all of life captive for Christ. We don't do that by hiding securely within our ecclesiastical fortress. Rather, we move into the disputed territory.

And I choose to call it "disputed" territory, not "enemy" territory. I confess that I often use the word *secular* in a negative way, because so much of what is secular is in conflict with the sacred. But in truth, a great share of the secular is neither good nor bad; not, at least, until we make it so. Mother's Day or Independence Day can be reduced to something utterly devoid of God, and even to something in subtle competition with God. But the same can happen with our sacred days, as indicated by the contemporary move to Christmas cards that have reduced "Merry Christmas" (almost innocuous enough of itself) into the utterly bland "Season's Greetings" or "Happy Holidays." I repeat, secular days are of themselves neither good nor bad. But natural inertia will make them bad, while intentional effort is required to make them good.

Two courses, it seems to me, are open to us. The first is to see what legitimate relationship there may be between the lection and the secular emphasis of the day. Obviously, one shouldn't distort a passage to honor a day. But sometimes we miss some of the potential of a given passage simply because we insist on looking at it as we always have. We're satisfied to take that which is on the surface (what I call "strip-mining a text") instead of studying it long enough to see some of its further relationships or applications.

The other course is simply to leave the lectionary for a Sunday. It will still be there when you return, and you may be the better for your brief trip elsewhere. The lectionary is a magnificent instrument, but it should be a guide and an aid, not a master. It is the product of devout and able persons. But you, too, are devout and able, at least on your better days, so be willing occasionally to let the Spirit of God speak to you beyond the boundaries of the lectionary. I find no evidence that the Holy Spirit is confined within the lectionary, though I'm quite sure that the Holy Spirit is pleased to use it.

The sum of the matter is this: biblical faith has had a stake in the calendar from the beginning. Because we are eternal creatures, living just now within some boundaries of time, we have peculiar respect for time; and because this is so, we insist on elevating pieces of time to quasi-eternal status. Even the most secular and apparently irreligious people do so, because we cannot do otherwise. We refuse to let time be a flat plain; we insist that it be marked by peaks of significance. Furthermore, we aren't satisfied with the peaks nature has built in; new moons and seasons aren't enough. So we raise up peaks of our own. Some are religious, in every culture. And of course, many are national or patriotic. Some, like Labor Day, celebrate human progress, and others, like Valentine's Day, rejoice in human love. And some, like Groundhog Day, are just fun. Well, they may have begun as superstition, but mostly, they're fun.

But I don't think I stretch the point when I insist that there's some intimation of eternity in all these lively excursions in time, in our putting red-letter days into our calendars. And it's up to the preacher to make the most of the matter: in the case of

sacred days, to be sure their sacredness is more fully compre-
hended by the people of God, and in the case of the secular, to
invest them with the sacred potential that is their due.

NOTES

1. Bonnie Blackburn and Leofranc Holford-Strevens, *The
   Oxford Book of Days* (Oxford: Oxford University Press, 2000),
   v–vi.

1

New Year's Sunday

New Year's Day isn't a church holiday for Christians, and that's surprising. This is an instance where, unfortunately, we didn't follow the example of our Jewish forebears. For the Jew, Rosh Hashanah, New Year's Day, is one of the high holy days. On that day, according to Jewish tradition, all the inhabitants of the world file before God for judgment. But this is seen as a merciful judgment, not a sealed one. S. Y. Agnon reminds us that the purpose of this yearly review on Rosh Hashanah is that our "sins may not grow too numerous."[1]

The ancient rabbis felt that this day assured the world of survival, because without it our sins would accumulate to the point of dooming the world. What the rabbis taught as a fact of the universe I think many of us feel as a truth of the psyche. The world may not collapse if we don't do something about our sins, but our individual lives will fall apart, or become so insensitive as to lose any profound humanness.

Obviously, the Jewish sense of awe is missing from our popular celebration of the New Year. All of us feel the need for a new start, and—as much as possible—with a clean slate. We like the sense of beginning again, the optimism that says, "This time I'll do better." I'm altogether certain that each of us needs this feeling of starting again. Theologically, there's little need to make the point, and yet it's worth recalling the words of Henry Sloane Coffin. A great pastor at Madison Avenue Presbyterian

Church for many years, then for nineteen years president of New York's Union Theological Seminary, he once observed that there is probably not "a more comforting text in the entire Bible than this: 'Our God is a consuming fire.' What a guarantee it gives us for a clean earth!"[2] Indeed! And every one of us has such a need within. The garbage of life weighs us down if we do not find time and place to deal with it; the garbage not only of our sins but also of our fruitless regrets and our "if onlys." We need encouragements for beginning again, and New Year's Day provides such a mood.

But a Christian sermon must get beyond easy moralizing or a secular collection of resolutions. We need a very profound sense of forgiveness and grace. And the roots for these feelings must be grounded in Scripture. Resolutions come and go, and so do hopeful affirmations and gimmicks of positive thinking. Such superficial preaching gives a bad name to sermons for New Year's Sunday. We need a foundation in Scripture and doctrine.

A great many churches that do not celebrate Holy Communion regularly nevertheless do so on the first Sunday of January. This, too, is a particular means of grace, and if the service includes such a ritual, the preacher will want to bring it into the sermon by direct reference. In truth, we can never remind worshipers enough that the sacrament is a saving ordinance. Whether Communion is celebrated frequently or seldom, too many worshipers celebrate it in a sadly superficial way. This isn't entirely the preacher's fault; superficiality is part of our human defense against painful growth. But we can do something about it by reminding our congregants of what may seem obvious.

So let the preacher approach the first Sunday of the year (or in some instances, the last Sunday of the old year) with gratitude and anticipation: gratitude, because the day makes so many persons more sensitive to the possibility of new commitments; and anticipation, because so many good things can happen. And let the preacher also remember that if this day is not grasped for its worth, a full year will go by before there is again such a strategic opportunity.

The sermon that follows was preached in a county-seat town, Versailles, Kentucky, as part of an early January weekend of spiritual renewal. I tried to bring together the feeling of Christmas, Epiphany, and the New Year's longing for starting again.

* * * *

GOING HOME ANOTHER WAY

Scripture Lesson: Matthew 2:1–12

For almost as long as I can remember, I've felt a bond with the wise men. I'm sure this sounds presumptuous, and of course I don't mean it the way it sounds. I have no illusions of either wisdom or profound scholarship. I suppose it's simply that I got acquainted with the wise men rather early, and that this early acquaintance was, in its own right, a glamorous one.

In the two small churches of my childhood, we had Christmas pageants no matter how shallow the pool of talent. That meant that some of us were drafted early into major roles. Because I was big for my age and began to have a bass voice when I was only nine, I became a wise man early, complete with whiskers, a bathrobe, grand headgear—ready to stride down the aisle singing, "We Three Kings of Orient Are."

It was some years before I realized that these three men were not kings but wise men; that they came not wearing crowns but with pens and scrolls. In my later years, I've come to realize that the wise men may have been very much like people in our twenty-first-century think tanks. They researched all kinds of data and gave counsel to rulers—and probably also to entrepreneurs and investors. This was before the age of specialization, so they were scientists, mathematicians, philosophers, theologians, economists, and political scientists, all rolled into one. I repeat, it was a long while before I realized that these strangers who came to see Jesus were not kings but wise men.

And it was even longer before I appreciated what they went through to see Jesus, and then to go home again—especially the going home again.

The Bible tells us next to nothing about them. It doesn't even tell us that there were three; we reach that conclusion because they had three gifts. We're told that they were "wise men from the East," who had seen a "star in the East" and had come to pay homage to the new king of the Jews.

Now think for a moment. What kind of wise men were they, to be out looking for a king of the Jews? The monarchy had disappeared six hundred years earlier, when the nation-state of Judah fell to Babylonia, and no one cared except the Jews. And for that matter, I'm not sure that all of the Jews cared; no doubt many of them had grown accustomed to a subsidiary role, as long as it meant reasonable security. Besides, when they had kings, most of them weren't that big a deal. Their kings weren't like Cyrus or Nebuchadnezzar or Alexander the Great. They weren't power brokers like the pharaohs of Egypt. Except for David and Solomon, they were pretty much nonentities on the international scene. And there hadn't been even a nonentity for six hundred years. So why in the world would these wise men, these people who did such arduous research, travel for weeks to meet a new king of the Jews?

Obviously, something out of the ordinary was driving these men. Perhaps the person who caught the mood best was T. S. Eliot, felt by many to have been the greatest poet of the twentieth century. Eliot seeks to get inside the wise men as he ponders the cities, towns, and villages en route where they were sometimes exploited, sometimes treated with hostility; and through it all, a wondering in their hearts if their whole journey was nothing but folly.[3]

I'm sure of it, very sure of it: they must often have heard voices telling them their trip was all folly. It was a long, long journey, over often difficult terrain. When they got to Palestine, they did a quite logical thing, which was also quite foolish. They went to the capital city, Jerusalem, to find the new king. As I said, this was logical enough, because that's where a king is ordinarily to be found. But it was also foolish, because the only king to be found was Herod the Great, appointed king of the Jews by Rome some forty years earlier.

When King Herod learned that a king had been born to the Jews, he was frightened. Herod was psychotic about his throne; he killed several members of his own family for fear they might take the throne from him. He didn't reveal his feelings to the wise men, of course. Instead, he made what seemed to be a quite solicitous appeal: when the wise men found the king, would they please bring the word back to him so he could pay proper homage? His intention, of course, was to arrange for the infant to be killed.

Well, as you know from watching dozens of Christmas pageants, the wise men found Jesus. Unless those wise men were driven by more than earthly wisdom, they had to be bewildered by what they found. Here was what appeared to be an ordinary Jewish baby, with obviously ordinary parents. The mother was a peasant girl; anyone could see that. Radiant, yes, and perhaps with a remarkable aura of goodness—but just a peasant girl. As Matthew's Gospel reports the story, only Mary and the baby were there at the time. We don't know if the wise men ever saw Joseph. If they did, they would have seen a laborer; you could tell by looking at his hands, his shoulders, his strong upper torso. A good man to know if you're going to build a house, but not the sort you expect to sire a king.

But somehow, against all odds, the wise men knew they had found the king of the Jews. So they brought out their store— gold, frankincense, and myrrh—and laid it at the child's feet. The gifts seemed inappropriate for this child; he was more in need of a blanket, or perhaps a new swaddling cloth. But they were captured at the heart, so they gave the infant their extravagant gifts.

And now they must get the word back to Herod, just as he had asked them to do. But the Bible says that they were "warned in a dream not to return to Herod, [so] they left for their own country by another road" (Matthew 2:12). It was a dangerous thing to do. Within Herod's own borders, he was a powerful man, and maniacally mean. He took no thought of any human life that stood in the way of his wishes. And even if the wise men escaped Herod and were once again safe in their homeland, Herod could still cause them trouble. As I see it, the wise men probably made much of their living by serving as consultants and counselors to rulers. If that's your work, you don't want bad references to begin circulating among your prospective clients—and Herod's references were surely going to be bad ones!

But they went home another way. That's how thoroughly the wise men had come to believe in this infant. They chose another route than the convenient, familiar, and shortest one. They put their future and their lives in peril because they believed this infant was supremely special.

When the Bible says that the wise men returned to their own country by another way, it's talking in terms of geography and road maps and travel plans. But of course there's more to it. The reason they took another way home is that they were now taking another way in their hearts. These were not the same men who came to Bethlehem. They came as scholars, political consultants, and men on a quest for power. They went home transformed.

How transformed? We'll never know. But transformed enough that they gambled their careers and their very lives on what they had seen. I turn again to T. S. Eliot. In his poem, the wise men are reminiscing over their journey years later. They ask themselves if their long journey had really led them to a place of birth, or perhaps to a place of death. They knew well enough that they had encountered a birth; they could remember the baby they had seen. But there was also a death: "Hard and bitter agony for us, like Death, our death,"[4]

T. S. Eliot was right, of course. The wise men died when they saw Jesus. That's why they had to go home another way. If they were the same when they left as when they came, they would have gone back to Herod. But those men died. They were new men now, and they had to go home another way.

Now hear me. Christmas doesn't mean very much unless it causes us to go home another way. If the wise men had gone home the way they came, it would have been just as well if they had missed Christmas altogether. And that, it seems to me, is the tragedy of Christmas as we too often know it and practice it.

Most of us do a reasonably good job of celebrating Christmas. Mind you, there's far, far too much commercialism, and far too much loose conduct at some Christmas parties, and too much superficial sentimentality at much of what happens in church. But on the whole it isn't too bad. We get caught up in good things: in giving and in friendship; in singing and laughter; in talk about peace on earth and doing things for other people. That's all nice, and even when we do it rather poorly, we look good doing it. Like the wise men, we do a pretty good job of coming to the manger with our gifts. We don't always know what we're doing, but we do pretty well; and as I've already indicated, the wise men probably didn't know what they were doing, either, when at first they came. So we do reasonably well at celebrating Christmas.

But we don't do so well at *going home another way*. We leave the Christmas scene too much as when we came. Believe me, there ought to be some dying at Christmastime. Because if we really meet our Lord Christ, some things in our lives will have to die. I won't try to be specific, because the Holy Spirit can make better application for you and for me than I can. But I know that, like the wise men, something in us has to die when we come to acknowledge Jesus' birth.

Today, thanks be to God, the calendar is on our side—not only the church calendar, which directs our attention to Epiphany and the coming of the wise men, but the civil calendar and the start of another year. There could hardly be a better time to see some old parts of us die and to set out on this new journey "another way." The prospect of another way is always upon us, but it comes to us with particular power as we set a new calendar on the desk or the wall.

I suspect that at this moment someone is muttering quietly, "I thought we were done with Christmas a week ago." I understand. And that's our problem. We may be done with Christmas, but Christmas isn't done with us. Not until we're ready to go home *another way*. And blessed be God, we're at an ideal place for beginning the journey. It's a new year; and by God's grace, a wonderful place to start again.

NOTES

1. Shmuel Yosef Agnon, *Days of Awe* (New York: Schocken Books, 1965), 15.
2. Henry Sloane Coffin, *Joy in Believing* (New York: Charles Scribner's Sons, 1956), 4.
3. T. S. Eliot, "Journey of the Magi," in *The Complete Poems and Plays, 1909–1950* (New York: Harcourt, Brace and Company, 1959), 68.
4. Ibid., 69.

2

Valentine's Day

We don't usually think of Valentine's Day as a religious holiday, or even a potentially religious one. It has some verified religious roots, however, and long-standing ones at that. The ancient Romans had a lovers' festival known as the feast of Lupercalia, named for Lupercus, their fertility god. Its elements were structured for pleasant, low-key courting; the aim was romance.

In 496, Pope Gelasius tried to co-opt this day for the church, just as the ancient church did with so many other pagan events. He changed the name to Saint Valentine's Day and the date from February 15 to February 14, but the sentiment stayed. There's dispute, however, as to who Saint Valentine was.

Now the event is pretty thoroughly staked out by the candy, greeting-card, florist, and restaurant interests. Ordinarily, the closest the contemporary church gets to the celebration is a dinner sponsored by the Couples' Club. But there are preaching possibilities here, and we should take them.

If the occasion is a pleasant church dinner of the kind I've just mentioned, the pastor is likely to be asked to "give a talk." The program committee means it to be just that: not a full-orbed sermon but something warm, light, humorous, and a little sentimental. And there's nothing wrong with that. The talk ought to have a bit of substance woven into its pleasantries, but they ought to stand on their own quality, without undue preachiness. One should be especially careful not to hurt the

recently widowed or the divorced who happen to come to the
event (our church occasions have a well-intentioned way of
becoming clumsily inclusive). In truth, it isn't difficult to draw
laughs at an occasion of this kind, or to give folks a generally
warm feeling; the setting itself, the table decorations, and the
special music make it easy to laugh. But it is really quite difficult to do this job so well that it might be redemptive or faith-
building. Mind you, I don't suppose it has to be. Common grace
might suggest that it's enough simply to increase people's general feeling of well-being. But our culture has so few opportunities for redemption and faith building that I like to gain a yard
or two any time someone hands me the ball.

But suppose Valentine's Day falls on Sunday—or even Saturday or Monday. Shall a preacher take advantage of the day
and, like Pope Gelasius, try to convert it? I think it's worth a try,
building on my basic conviction that we ought to take full
advantage of the calendar, whether sacred, secular, or semi-
sacred. The sermon that follows is an attempt to do so. It was
preached to a rather average congregation but somewhat dis-
proportionately leaning to people in their sixties and over.

* * * *

HEARTS AND FLOWERS

Scripture Lesson: Luke 11:14–28

Press me just a bit, and I'll confess that I'm a sentimental person. My eyes are likely to brim at an old Jimmy Stewart movie such as *Mr. Smith Goes to Washington,* and I may never get over Peter O'Toole's handling of *Good-bye, Mr. Chips.* I'm ready to listen to those stories about the dog that won't leave its master's grave, and my heart beats fast when a band plays "Stars and Stripes Forever." No doubt about it, I'm sentimental.

But I also know that sentiment can be superficial—what we sometimes call "cheap sentiment." I realize that it's possible to use sentiment to avoid dealing with life at some of its deeper, more compelling levels. That may be especially true in the realm of religion, because religion is in so many ways a matter of the heart.

But because I'm sentimental, I think I would have been upset with Jesus if I had been with him one day, as he and his disciples traveled toward Jerusalem. Let me tell you what happened.

Jesus had just cast out a demon, so that a person who had previously been mute was now able to speak. This person was apparently not deaf, just mute; perhaps it was some variation on what we today call autism, or perhaps some severe emotional trauma that had paralyzed the person's ability to speak. In any event, Jesus set the person free, so that he or she could now speak. It was an awesome moment.

But immediately, some of the enemies of Jesus said that he had worked this miracle by the power of the devil. A vigorous discussion followed, as Jesus challenged his opponents. As you read the story, you can feel the tension in the crowd, and you can almost hear Jesus raise his voice in a mixture of scorn and anger. As I observe the scene, I'm appalled that these people resented Jesus so much that even when a person had been healed, they would make the healing an issue of controversy instead of rejoicing in the person's good fortune. If I had been there, I would have been disgusted that our Lord's enemies could be so hard-hearted. Their hatred seems almost demonic.

And as I read the story, something else bothers me even more. Why doesn't someone speak in Jesus' defense? I'd like to hear an "Amen" from the crowd when Jesus replies so skillfully to his opponents. Where is Peter at this moment? Peter is never reluctant to offer an opinion; why doesn't he say something now?

Then, suddenly, from the crowd, we hear a voice. It's a woman's voice—a bit shrill, quite emotional, and adoring. We're surprised to hear a woman speak out like this, because this first-century world is one in which women (to use a phrase) "knew their place," and kept it. But this woman, Luke tells us, "raised her voice" (Luke 11:27); and she raised it, it's very clear, in support of Jesus. Listen to her: "Blessed is the womb that bore you and the breasts that nursed you" (Luke 11:27).

Be honest with me. Are you a bit startled by what the woman has said? It's interesting, isn't it, that, living in a world where television takes us into someone's bedroom half a dozen times every evening, we're nevertheless somewhat embarrassed when we hear this woman refer to the breast and the womb in a truly appropriate way.

As a matter of fact, this woman is rather poetic. All she was trying to say was "Your mother is a lucky woman, to have a son like you!" But she puts it in picture language, like a natural poet. Perhaps her words were a folk phrase in those days. In any event, she chose her words well, and I am moved by them. And I'm moved even more by her courage. Someone in that crowd needed to say that she was on Jesus' side, and this peasant woman did so. She did so in the language and perceptions of a first-century woman, and I want to applaud her.

But Jesus turns and picks up her very word, *blessed*, and says, "Blessed rather are those who hear the word of God and obey it" (Luke 11:28)!

This isn't the answer I expect from Jesus. I expect him to pause, look gratefully at the woman, and say, "And blessings on you, too, good woman!" Instead, he speaks what seems very much like a rebuke. In truth, Jesus is saying something like "This is no time for sentiment. Get with it, woman."

This isn't the way I want Jesus to respond. Jesus, who finds time at the well of Samaria to visit at great length with a rather disreputable woman; Jesus, who prevents religious leaders from stoning a woman taken in adultery; Jesus, who cares about a timid woman who simply wants to touch the hem of his robe— we don't expect this Jesus to brush aside a simple woman's well-meaning sentiment.

And we're especially surprised at where we find this story. The four Gospel writers, Matthew, Mark, Luke, and John, have their own points of emphasis, but except for John, in a majority of cases they report on something that at least one or two of the others has said. And when a Gospel writer is alone in telling a story, we figure there's a reason. Luke is the only writer who tells the little incident about this woman. But here's the irony. Luke's Gospel is notably sensitive to women. Luke seems, in this regard, like an old-fashioned family doctor. So I'm surprised that Luke, of all people, would include this story and tell it as he has, in what sounds like a put-down of this woman.

But something else may be bothering you. You know that today is Valentine's Day, the day of hearts and flowers, of candy and roses and lovely sentiments. So you want to ask me, "What kind of subject is *this* for Valentine's Day?"

And I have to answer, "The best of subjects!" Because in order to live life the way God wants it lived, you've got to have heart—"miles and miles and miles of heart." But it needs to be the kind of heart, the very big kind of heart, the Bible recommends.

You see, we use the word *heart* somewhat differently from the way the Bible does. We think of the heart as the center of our emotions, but when the biblical writers spoke of their emotions, they were likely to refer to their bowels or their kidneys; the way we do, come to think of it, when we speak of emotions that "tie our stomachs in knots," or when we say that someone is so deeply in love as to have lost their appetite.

But what about the heart? As I understand it, the Bible thinks of the heart as a kind of combination of feelings, thought, and will. It's far, far more than just feelings; it's feelings informed by thinking and by commitments. The Bible uses the word *heart* literally hundreds of times, but not simply as a description of the emotions. It's a bigger, tougher word than that.

I think that's the mood in which Jesus responded to this well-meaning, earnest woman. Sentiment is wonderful; it has its place. But if sentiment is to make a difference in life, it must get a tough inner core of quality. Otherwise it will soon be nothing more than warm, fuzzy feelings.

If you've read the Gospel of Luke somewhat carefully, you know that at this point in the story, Jesus is on his rather long journey to Jerusalem for the series of events that will lead to his crucifixion. The distance traveled is not long—certainly not by our modern measure—but its events and conversations extend over more than half of this Gospel. As I read Luke, I'm impressed that a certain urgency, bordering even on impatience, marks our Lord's conduct and his teaching. He knows that a cross lies ahead. Notice, then, Jesus' demanding words and deeds: the barren fig tree, the narrow door, the parable of the dinner invitations that were rejected, the cost of discipleship. So when this kind woman says a lovely, sentimental thing (a kind of Valentine's Day greeting)—"Blessed is the womb that bore you and the breasts that nursed you"—Jesus seems to answer that her words aren't enough. There's a cross up ahead, and a showdown with hell. "Blessed rather are those who hear the word of God and obey it." This is the quality of commitment Jesus needs now from his disciples, and I suspect he senses that he's not going to get it.

What Jesus said is dramatically appropriate to our own day. Hollywood and the novelist are saying, "Blessed are those who fall in love!" Life answers, as Jesus warned us, "Blessed, rather, are those who stay in love." Television says, "How lucky are those who slip into bed on their first meeting." Jesus answers, "How lucky are those who establish a relationship of integrity and honor that will carry them through the unpredictable vagaries of life." I stood in a travelers' service line not long ago near a striking couple in their thirties. I watched their faces; I do a good deal of face watching. The woman's eyes had that special feminine capacity for adoration, but at this moment she was looking at her husband with exasperation that bordered on anger and contempt. I asked myself when it was that the look of adoring love had given way to the look of disgusted impatience. I think it was somewhere between sentiment and reality, between Valentine's Day and carrying out the garbage.

The same issue shows itself all through our common days. We are terribly susceptible to superficial standards, standards that are as shallow as sin and as broad-minded as hell. We find it so easy to confuse matters by superficial sentiment—in government, in politics, in the raising of our children, in the issues of the workplace. We're afraid to say that something is wrong, lest we seem "judgmental." I'll confess readily that I've known enough judgmental people in my life, and have often enough been judgmental myself, that I recognize the danger. I know that we all make mistakes, and we are all sinners; I know it well. But that doesn't mean that you and I should endorse mistake making or wink at sin. We dare not allow soft-hearted sentimentalism to degenerate into soft-headed thinking; nor should we allow our well-meaning broad-mindedness to become an attitude that says, "Anything goes."

When that woman spoke out from the crowd so long ago, "Blessed is the womb that bore you and the breasts that nursed you," she was—it seems to me—the first recorded person to honor and revere the Virgin Mary, mother of Jesus. That gives her a quite remarkable place in human history in general, and in church history in particular.

But Jesus said, "Blessed rather are those who hear the word of God and obey it." Isn't that quite astonishing? If we take our Lord's words at face value, as I suspect we should, we should pause for a moment when we pass a church that is named for the Virgin Mary, or when we hold in hand a symbol or medal of the Virgin, and we should say, "If I *hear* the word of God, and *obey* it, I am more blessed than the one who held the Son of God to her bosom."

So, on this Valentine's Day, if you say to some person—or for that matter, to some cause, or even to your church—"I love you with all of my heart," ask yourself about the size of your heart. Are our hearts cozy little places of sentiment, or are they the totality of our being? Are our feelings just hearts and flowers or the stuff that sustains life through the long pull?

This is a question for Valentine's Day. It's also a question for all of life. Sentiment is a good thing; it nurtures the tender side of our personalities, and it often causes us to do gracious, loving things. But life in general and the Christian life in particular demand more than warm feelings. With the cross that so often looms ahead in our world, we need a quality of life that will compel us to hear the word of God and obey it. When we do, we are blessed in a way that exceeds even the blessing that was given to the mother of our Lord.

3

Ash Wednesday

Ash Wednesday is one of my favorite church holidays. Some may think this affection somewhat morbid, since Ash Wednesday is a day marked by repentance and soul searching, and even by fasting. But for me, it's a day of excitement; because Ash Wednesday is the beginning of Lent, and when I was a pastor I looked forward to the Lenten season. A typical congregation, like an average Christian, needs times of renewal, and Lent provides such a time. The churches I knew as a boy found those times of renewal in revival services or times of "deeper life" emphasis. As a pastor of churches with no such revival tradition, I found that Lent provided the same opportunity in a somewhat different form. And Lent begins with Ash Wednesday.

I suppose it could be said that Ash Wednesday is a manufactured holy day. It isn't related to a particular person, nor to a particular event in the life of our Lord. The date is established by counting back forty days from Easter, not including Sundays. Why forty? Because forty is the classical, biblical number for testing, trial, or judgment. Specifically, these forty days remind us of the days of testing Jesus spent in the wilderness just after his baptism.

Ash Wednesday, or more classically the Day of Ashes, gets its name from the practice of marking a cross in ashes on the foreheads of the faithful. The celebration of this day began sometime in the tenth century. I suspect its origins may have come from a setting of deep piety, where priest or people were looking for new venues of adoration and commitment; or perhaps from a time of spiritual malaise, when some church leader was searching for a device that would stimulate spiritual renewal in the populace. Whatever its origins, Ash Wednesday continues to elicit mixed support. Some come with deep longing, praying that in this Lenten season they will find the deeper walk with Christ that their souls so earnestly desire. Others treat the day as a religious formality, perhaps even with some touches of superstition, expecting nothing more than the observance of a ritual. I have come, over the years, to be grateful for even religious formalities, recognizing that sometimes the Spirit of God uses perfunctory observances as a means of renewal.

On occasions such as Ash Wednesday, we pastors do well to remember that language commonplace to us may be foreign to our people. We are wise, therefore, to explain, whether in the course of the homily or in the church bulletin or newsletter, something of the meaning of the day: of ashes as an ancient symbol of loss and repentance; of the historic words spoken during the imposition of the ashes, "Remember that thou art dust, and to dust thou shalt return"; of the practice in many religious communions of using ashes made from the palms of the previous year's Palm Sunday; and, of course, that the imposition of the ashes is a sign of mourning and of repentance.

We sometimes reason that because we explained all these matters last year or at some other fairly recent time, it is superfluous to do it again. Not so. Our people have been occupied with several other matters in the meanwhile. Repetition is essential to good teaching.

I first preached this sermon when a United Methodist church in Barbourville, Kentucky, asked me to speak for their Ash Wednesday service. Some years later I repeated it, with some renewal and revision, for a United Church of Christ congregation in Lakewood, a suburb of Cleveland, Ohio. On the surface, the congregations were very different: a small county-seat town in the Kentucky mountains versus a middle-class sub-urb of a northern industrial city. But below the surface were the same human need for God and the same basic longing for a more fulfilling life in Christ.

* * * *

ALL FALL DOWN

Scripture Lesson: Romans 3:9–12, 22–24

Ash Wednesday is one of the most solemn days in all the church calendar, so you may well wonder what's on my mind when I say that I want to talk with you about playing games. But there's some logic to what I'm about—perhaps the logic of contrast. We speak often of life as a game, even when we're talking about the deadly seriousness of it. And we speak of "the race of life" and of the kind of life that finds its description in the phrase "the loneliness of the long-distance runner." The apostle Paul liked the game theme. He described the Christian life as a race, with a victor's crown at the end. When he felt his own life was near its end, he resorted to two game figures in one sentence: "I have fought the good fight, I have finished the race" (2 Timothy 4:7).

But I'm going a bit farther; perhaps you'll feel I'm stretching the matter to the absurd. I'm thinking specifically about a children's game. There may be some natural poignancy in many of the images that come to us from the world of sports, so that they seem worthy of such a time as Ash Wednesday. But not mine—at least, not at first. Listen:

> Ring around a rosey,
> A pocket full of posies;
> Ashes, ashes . . .
> All fall down.

The game is several hundred years old; no one knows its age for sure. It has crossed the Atlantic Ocean, from its probable birthplace in England, and I have no doubt it has also crossed the Pacific, to say nothing of the Mediterranean. Children play it around the world.

No one knows for sure what the chant means. Some scholars have said that the words refer to the period of the great epidemics, when faces would be marked by rosy rings, but that theory has been pretty well discredited. For that matter, who knows how the words have changed since first they were spoken? And still more, who would dare suggest that mere adults could ever fully understand what children are thinking about when they play? Children's games are often a strange mix of laughter and seriousness, because children work at their play. They won't find out until later that play is for relaxation; they see games as the very business of their lives, so even with their laughter, they go about their games quite seriously—which, come to think of it, is like the way some adults play golf or bridge.

But "Ring around the Rosey" has a unique emphasis on the serious-laughter theme, because it ends each round with the children singing, "Ashes, ashes, all fall down," at which point the children do just that: they fall down in a heap of mock distress, mixed with laughter.

And that's the image in my mind on this Ash Wednesday: human beings in this endless game of life, this generation-after generation game, tumbling all we can, "Ashes, ashes, we all fall down."

Ash Wednesday, as you know, is the day that opens the Lenten season. Lent itself is meant to be a time of self-examination and penitence, and Ash Wednesday sets the tone. For generations, Roman Catholic churches and many Episcopal congregations have followed a simple, rather poignant ceremony—one that is now being observed by an increasing number of general Protestant bodies. The faithful come to church on the morning of Ash Wednesday (and in many Protestant churches later in the day), and the priest smudges a bit of ash on the forehead. In communities with large Catholic populations, you see the sign all around you as you hurry to work. The ash on the forehead is a badge of confession and of repentance. If I may say so, it is a badge that announces, "Ashes, ashes, we all fall down."

Ashes are an ancient biblical symbol of sin, shame, and remorse. You find the reference perhaps a dozen times in the Old Testament. When persons felt life had caved in on them, or that they had lost all their friends, or that they were separated from God, they would clothe themselves in rough sackcloth, then throw ashes over their bodies and into their hair.

The symbolism is vivid; so vivid, it hardly needs explaining. Ashes speak to us of destruction and loss—total loss. If a family suffer a fire, they'll almost surely say, "Everything's gone. All we have to show are the ashes." The idea is so powerful that we use that phrase not only for loss by fire but for any kind of loss—the end of a friendship, perhaps, or the failure of a business. We speak the ashes theme at the graveside, as the last earthly remains are lowered into their resting place: "Earth to earth, ashes to ashes, dust to dust." We use the term poetically when we say, "My dreams have turned to ashes." When life crashed in on that good man Job, he at last sat down on an ash heap to scrape his boils. There must have been better places to sit, and surely more comfortable ones, but an ash heap seemed to Job the most appropriate setting. Later, when he complained to God about his piteous circumstances, he said,

> [God] has cast me into the mire,
>   and I have become like dust and ashes.
>   (Job 30:19)

Let me venture an opinion; I can't prove it, but I'm very sure of it. I suspect you can go anywhere in the world and you'll find that ashes are a symbol of loss, of despair, of heartbreak, and of repentance. And I venture it has been that way since our human ancestors first got hold of fire and found that it was—if controlled—one of their greatest benefits; and therefore, when it died, or when it got out of control, the ashes spoke in sullen and dramatic terms of the extent of their loss.

No wonder, then, that our spiritual ancestors in Christendom used ashes as a symbol for the beginning of the season of repentance, and that we've been doing so for over a thousand years. If you feel sorry for your sins, and if it seems to you that you have burned up some of the best of life so that now all you have to show for yourself are some ashes—ah, then, ashes belong on the forehead.

And who, please tell me, can feel otherwise? Is there any one of us who can say that we've never sullied life? That astute student of human nature, the apostle Paul, put it sharply and all-inclusively: "all have sinned and fall short of the glory of God" (Romans 3:23).

There is no one who is righteous,
    not even one;
there is no one who has understanding,
there is no one who seeks God.
                    (Rom. 3:10–11)

We *all fall down*. In this game of life, this ring around the rosey, we all fall down. Sometimes when children play the game, someone obstinately remains standing, at which point all the other children say, "That's not fair! You don't understand the game. We *all* fall down." When I see some adult who thinks he or she is still standing, who is offended that the Communion service includes a confession of sin, I want to say, "You don't understand this game: not life, nor sin, nor even your own self. We fall down. We *all* fall down."

That remarkable Episcopal clergywoman Fleming Rutledge acknowledges that some will feel we talk too much about sin on a day like Ash Wednesday. But she goes on to observe that some traits of our character—in truth, expressions of sin—are "so tenaciously imbedded in human personality that we scarcely think about them."[1] No wonder we find it hard to abide by the rules of the game, to confess that *we all fall down*.

In most liturgical churches, we get the ashes for Ash Wednesday by burning the palms that were used the previous year in the Palm Sunday processional. Whoever started such a tradition was wonderfully on target. The ashes of our lives are developed not only in the times of our grievous misdoings but sometimes in our high moments of celebration, and even in the midst of our best religious declarations. We shout, "Hosanna," and we mean it. But somehow we find it difficult to make the "Hosanna" of Sunday carry through the routine of Tuesday or the trial on Thursday or Friday. Yes, it's dramatically significant that the ashes for our day of repentance come from the palm leaves of our exuberant religious celebration.

There's so much pathos in our ring around the rosey. We enter our happy little game, laughing together around a dinner table with friends. The circle moves ever more rapidly as conversation picks up; then, without warning, you speak a word that you know cuts a friend, a sweetheart, a spouse. Perhaps you hurry past it, hoping no one noticed, or you try to draw it back. But now you realize it's too late; anything you do will only exacerbate the pain. The word has been spoken, the harm done; several faces flush with embarrassment and tension. Afterward you say, "How could I ever have been so insensitive, so stupid? How could I have said such a thing?"

Sometimes the game takes longer to develop. We do a relatively innocent thing and are able still to go about our rosy circle. But one day the innocent thing—or the *nearly* innocent thing—becomes a habit, then a binding vice, so that we not only fall down, we can no longer imagine a way to rise. Indeed, we may no longer even desire to rise.

Sometimes the game plays itself out in our minds. On the outside, we walk a straight line, or at least follow a proper minuet. But within, the mind races all around the rosey, with thoughts of lust perhaps, or anger, or crude ambition, or desire for revenge. No one knows the game our minds are playing, while our faces and conduct are quite proper. But believe me, we can't fool this game of life. There is God, at last, with whom we must deal. And yes, we must also deal with ourselves, because as our unworthy thoughts accumulate, they insist on their toll. Deep inside they eat away—not only at the conscience and the spiritual life but also at our bodies and our minds, until we grow sick at one or both.

That's why we need Ash Wednesday—because we all fall down. We sin and come short of the glory of God. And in our ashes we begin the act of repentance before God.

You understand, of course, that Ash Wednesday is not the only time we should confess our mortality and repent. This ought to be a daily act, so that we keep confessed-up before God. But Ash Wednesday dramatizes the need and provides a particularly apt setting for our repentance—and with it, new hope.

Several years ago, the Roman Catholic churches of Lexington, Kentucky, ran a large advertisement at the beginning of a Lenten season, giving the location of their churches and urging attendance. They titled the page "From Ashes to Easter." That's a true and lovely statement of our journey. We begin with the ashes of our failures, our mistakes, our sins, and our need, but we move on to the grand deliverance of Easter. And again, this is true not only of the seasonal celebration but also of the trivial and the profound business of daily life. We have our ashes, our falling down, but thanks be to God, we have Easter. Our Lord has won the game.

I think I wouldn't want to preach on Ash Wednesday if there were not the prospect of Easter. I couldn't bear to announce that we "all fall down" if the story ended there. Ours is a better ring around the rosey. Ashes and all, we rise up to start anew. For we are a resurrection people, blessed with new life in Christ, and we must remember this, even as we repent on Ash Wednesday. We all fall down, but by God's grace we can rise to start anew.

NOTES

1. Fleming Rutledge, *Help My Unbelief* (Grand Rapids: Wm. B. Eerdmans Publishing Co., 2000), 130–31.

4

April Fools' Day

Can anything good come out of April Fools' Day? Why not? By its nature it's a jolly sort of day, and it demands that we not take ourselves too seriously. In my mind, anything that keeps us from being overly serious about ourselves has much to commend it. I recall that little boys sometimes used to invest a little nastiness into their celebration of the day, and occasionally some adults stretch the boundaries of good taste; but on the whole, the unfortunate thing about this holiday is that we don't have enough fun with it. I still smile when I remember the year National Public Radio broke the news that Starbucks was planning, at a cost of untold millions, to build a coffee pipeline all across America, so that all the coffee served in their outlets would come directly from Seattle. And I enjoyed even more the year NPR featured a brief interview with the great Yo-Yo Ma, in which he announced that he was giving up the cello (had found it boring, as I recall) and would thereafter devote his musical gifts and energy to the accordion.

As I note in the sermon that follows, this little holiday came into existence over four hundred years ago in France, as the result of a change in the calendar. People ever since have used the day as an excuse to play harmless jokes on one another. The celebration soon spread to England, then through the British Isles, and of course came to America with settlers from these countries. In France the victim of a joke is called an April *fish*, and in Scotland, an April *gowk*.

One probably isn't likely to preach to the April Fools' theme on a Sunday, because April 1 is likely to fall during Lent. Of course, when it falls on Low Sunday, or near thereto, the situation seems made to order. It's more likely that a pastor will play upon this day at a banquet on that day, rather than on a Sunday. But don't rule out Sunday. The unexpectedness of the theme can be part of its appeal.

I have recommended in our opening chapter that in our preaching we take full advantage of the calendar, both sacred and secular; if a day is on the minds of the people, make use of their interest. That's how I happened to speak on this theme to a church in Zanesville, Indiana. I had spoken there for several years, on one occasion or another, but when they contacted me in this particular year, the only Lenten date I had open was April 1. As soon as I promised to speak on that day, I decided to find a theme that would join naturally with the day.

As it happens, my sermon—though it starts at a cordial level—is a particularly serious one. This is itself a homiletical device. There is much to be said for using a friendly, homely, or humorous setting to launch a serious word. Because the hearers are caught off guard, they hear more clearly.

* * * *

FOOLS, APRIL AND OTHERWISE

Scripture Lesson: 1 Corinthians 1:18–31

April Fools' Day is a good time to remind ourselves that we are all fools in some measure or other, at some place or other, in one way or another. It's a good time to do a serious foolishness check, to see where it is that we're foolish and to decide where we want to invest our foolishness.

That sounds terribly serious for a foolish day. April Fools' Day was born in France, over four hundred years ago. France was the first nation to adopt the reformed calendar, in 1564. Until then, the New Year's celebration began on March 21 and climaxed on April 1. With the new calendar, New Year's Day was changed, of course, to January 1. Some people, however, still celebrated New Year's Day on April 1, so they were known as April fools. Well, I suppose a person looks foolish when he or she thinks the year begins on a day already three months into the year. Still, in another sense a new year begins for any particular person on that day when they let it begin. I'd rather celebrate New Year's Day on April 1 and really make a new start of my life than celebrate it on January 1 and do so like a fool.

Leo Stein said, "If all the fools were drowned in Noah's flood, the seed was saved."[1] You realize as much when you go to a carnival or a fair and see how people look for opportunities to be duped. Easier still, stay up late enough any night to catch some of those after-hour television commercials that promise an unbelievably amazing product that will cost only $19.95, plus $6.25 for postage and handling. There's still a thriving market in fools, no doubt about it.

But these are small-time fools. There are enough of them to grease the wheels of dubious industry, but their individual investments are small. The greater fools deal with greater matters, and they're not always easily recognized. Do you remember a popular song of some years ago, "What Kind of Fool Am I"? It was the cry of the lead character in a musical, a man who gave up love in order to get money and power and position. When it was all done, he asked himself what kind of fool he was, and why he couldn't "fall in love, like any other man." We play the fool when we sacrifice love in order to get money or power or prestige. Parents play the fool when they realize, after their children are grown and gone, that they've missed one of the greatest gifts this planet offers: the chance to grow up with their children. And they traded that chance for the opportunity to make money or to pursue social standing or to get the resources for a better house or more exotic vacations.

We can be fools in so many ways. For some of us, it's in the way we eat and drink. Some of us, as the saying goes, dig our graves with our teeth. Some play the fool with their hearts. There are women, and men, too, who make the same mistake over and over again, by falling in love with someone who will abuse or misuse them. One can play the fool with giftedness and talent. Some do so by letting the talent go wasted into the grave, while others employ their talent tirelessly, but in ways so selfish or so unworthy that it would have been better if they had never found it. And of course, we can be fools with our money and with our time. I suspect that for every person who plays the fool with money, there are a hundred who play the fool with time. That's especially sad, since time is our only irreplaceable resource.

So I repeat, all of us are fools now and then. It comes with the territory—the territory of humanness. Sometimes our foolish deeds are minor matters, the sort that make us say, "How could I ever have been so stupid?" But sometimes, Lord help us, we're fools in ways for which we pay with years of our lives. Some acts of foolishness follow us all the way to the grave. Yes, all the way to eternity.

And then there are those beautiful, wonderful, divinely inspired fools! There was that man long ago, named Saul of Tarsus. He came from a good family. Not only was he a Jew in the finest, purest tradition, but his father was of such attainments that Saul was born a Roman citizen. He was educated by one of the best scholars of his day, and while he was still a young man, he became a member of the most demanding and respected of religious bodies, the Pharisees.

But one day he was apprehended by Jesus Christ, and that changed everything. All those things I thought were so important, he said, I realized were nothing but garbage. And do you know what captured him? *Foolishness.* He said it himself. The message of the cross, he said, "is foolishness to those who are perishing" (1 Corinthians 1:18). And he was right. The cross was the most despised means of execution in that day or in any day; to die on a cross was to die in the most agonizing and shameful manner possible. But Paul had discovered that when Jesus Christ died on the cross, he had set loose in the world the power that saves eternally all who will accept it, and that will transform the living of life on this earth.

So Paul went everywhere playing the fool. They stoned him and left him for dead. Once he escaped only by being let over the wall in a basket, like a bundle of clothing. Another time his life was spared because his nephew overheard a plot against him. When he preached to the philosophers on Mars Hill, some laughed at him, though a few were converted. He made converts at Corinth, but they seemed at times to turn against him or to disregard his teachings. Three times he was shipwrecked while going about his missions, and five times he was beaten with thirty-nine stripes. Surely those who had known him as a brilliant young scholar must have said, "What a fool he's turned out to be."

But what a magnificent fool! If our world is to survive, if it is to move beyond its inertia, it will be because of fools like Paul.

I met such a fool just a few years ago, in his homeland, Bulgaria. The country was under the power of the old Soviet Union for forty years and was officially atheist for all that time. But this man, Zravko Breslov, insisted on preaching the Christian gospel and serving as a superintendent for the few Methodist congregations that managed to exist. When the Communist government tried to silence him, they found the only way they could do so was by imprisoning him. They broke his legs, and tried to break his spirit, but they found his spirit could not be broken as easily as his legs. For twelve years he was a prisoner. I was present on a September evening in 1989 when the World Methodist Council awarded Breslov its International Peace Prize. Two men helped him to the podium to receive the award. But after he had taken a firm hold on the pulpit, he was in command. He spoke forcefully; no wonder the Communist leaders were afraid of him. After all, what can one do with a fool who refuses to be intimidated? The award included a fairly large financial gift; large, certainly, for a man who had lived as simply as he had. Breslov accepted it with excitement and immediately gave it—every cent of it—to the Methodist church in Sophia, Bulgaria, to help them buy an organ. Such a fool, such a wonderful fool!

A fool must sometimes embrace the role. When Catherine Mumford married William Booth in 1855, she knew that he disapproved of women preaching. But one day in 1860, while sitting in her husband's church in Gateshead, England, she felt a compulsion to rise and speak. At the same time she sensed that if she did, she would surely make a fool of herself. In later years, Catherine loved to tell how she knew this to be the voice of the devil and replied, "That's just the point. I have never yet been willing to be a fool for Christ. Now I will be one."[2] In time, Catherine Booth became a powerful speaker, at one period addressing an average of one thousand persons a night for seventeen consecutive weeks.

A generation or two ago, the Anglican Church had a bishop in Zanzibar, Bishop Frank. He wanted above all to bring Jesus Christ to the people of Zanzibar. When he was back in England briefly, he asked another priest to join him in the work. The man excused himself. "I don't think I could live in Africa," he said. "I didn't ask you to live," Bishop Frank said. "You can glorify God by your death."[3]

Those are hard words, aren't they? Unreasonable words, as a matter of fact. But anything the church of Jesus Christ has done that has really mattered has come from persons who had just such deep convictions. This kind of faith operates at all levels and all frontiers of the Christian life. John Leax is a poet and a professor in a small Christian college in upstate New York. He has worked untiringly to keep a radioactive waste dump out of his area. At the end of several long months of heroic effort, Leax wrote, "What will come of our efforts to halt the siting of a dump in this valley, I do not know. I do not need to know. But this I do know. Christ is in the world, redeeming the world, and

I will name myself Christ's man as long as I have a breath to breathe his name."[4] Such a fool isn't compelled to win, to have the best odds, to be praised. There is something compelling, however, about having a conscience.

As I said earlier, everyone is a fool in some fashion or other. Some act like fools when they go to a party, and some at the height of a sporting event, like the Super Bowl or the NCAA basketball playoffs—which, come to think of it, the sports pages have christened "March Madness." The question is, whose fool will we be? What cause or excitement or object or person is worthy of our taking the "fool" title?

I'm pleading on this April Fools' Day for a kind of high commitment that our secular society really can't understand. It's the sort of commitment that causes some of us to do everything possible to lead our children to the Christian life. For others, it is the earnestness that makes us write the church into our budget every year, even while we may struggle to pay a mortgage, or at the price of a certain level of vacation. It is the kind of conviction that makes us be honest when we might gain some temporary advantage in our careers by cautiously cutting some corners.

And who knows where Christ is calling you or me, even now? It is never to paths of convenience; not for us. We follow one who chose to die like a fool, on a cross. He was driven by the conviction that the likes of you and me, and some still worse than we are, deserved to be saved, even by his death. It was quite clearly a foolish thing to do, an absurdity. The apostle Paul himself said so. As far as our world can see, Paul said, the cross is foolishness. But to those who experience it, it is the power of God.

In a time and in a culture where people are fools for so many reasons, I am more than ever persuaded to be a fool for Christ's sake. I warmly commend the same to you. And I tell you, if you will choose to be such a fool, you will find you have joined the very company of heaven. You will, by your choice, be part of the grandest body on our planet and in the precincts of eternity. God's fools! God's living, loving, faithful fools!

NOTES

1. Leo Stein, *Journey into the Self*, 154; quoted in *A Treasury of Jewish Quotations*, ed. Joseph L. Baron (South Brunswick, N. J.: Thomas Yoseloff, 1956), 127.
2. Roy Hattersley, *Blood and Fire* (New York: Doubleday, 2000), 113.
3. H. M. Smith, *Frank, Bishop of Zanzibar* (New York: Macmillan Co., 1926), 69.
4. John Leax, in *Stories for the Christian Year*, ed. Eugene H. Peterson (New York: Macmillan, 1992), 99.

5

Palm/Passion Sunday

We didn't know much about the liturgical calendar in the Protestantism of my Iowa boyhood, but somehow we knew about Palm Sunday. Perhaps what caught our attention was the simple drama the day encouraged, with the idea of children and palm branches, or perhaps the mood of victory implicit in the day provided relief from the demanding quality of everyday life in a world of limited economy. In any event we knew the day only as Palm Sunday, and if someone had suggested that we call it Passion Sunday, we would have heard them with incredulity.

But students of the liturgical calendar remind us that a congregation that goes from the triumph of Palm Sunday—fleeting and insubstantial as it is—to the grand triumph of Easter will miss the theological flow of our faith. Mind you, attendance at Maundy Thursday and Good Friday services would prevent such misunderstanding, but unfortunately, not that many church members attend these Holy Week services. So we do well to remember, and to be reminded, that the Sunday before Easter is not only the Sunday when we celebrate our Lord's triumphal entry into Jerusalem; it is, more particularly, the beginning of the week of Jesus' suffering. It is *Passion* Sunday.

The priest, whether Catholic, Episcopal, or Orthodox, may hope that the assembled worshipers on Passion Sunday understand the significance of the day. Pastors of most Protestant bodies can't be so sure. The popular weight of the day is toward

Palm Sunday, not Passion Sunday. Those who plan the celebration of the day and those who prepare the preaching should keep this in mind. They should not be taken captive by the Palm Sunday predisposition, but they should recognize that it exists, and should make this fact their ally. The preacher who chooses on this Sunday to chastise people for their benighted views about Palm Sunday, while insisting that they get the deeper meaning of preparation for passion week, may well prove a point but lose a pastoral opportunity.

Several emphases are appropriate to this particular Sunday, but the Palm Sunday factor should not be neglected and certainly should not be disparaged. Some years a pastor will want to emphasize the Palm Sunday elements, and sometimes those of Passion Sunday. But when the preacher goes to the Palm Sunday emphasis, he or she should be quite intentional about including some reference to the passion theme. I see no reason why the exuberance of Palm Sunday cannot rightly be included with the solemn challenge of the days just ahead in Holy Week. After all, much of the life we know has such pendulum swings. The pastor often goes from a Saturday morning funeral to an evening wedding, our hospital calls from rejoicing with parents of a newborn to quiet watching with those expecting the death of a loved one. Part of the extraordinary majesty of our faith is its sufficiency for all the seasons of life. The juxtaposition of Palm Sunday and Passion Sunday is appropriate to the faith we proclaim.

This sermon was first preached on April 4, 1993, at The Lost Tree Community Church, a gated community in North Palm Beach, Florida, and the following year in a somewhat revised form at the Centenary United Methodist Church in Lexington, Kentucky, a large suburban congregation. The Lost Tree congregation was made up largely of retired or semiretired persons, economically comfortable but with openness to their Christian responsibility. The Centenary church had a full range of ages but tended to be middle-class and upper-middle-class in its socioeconomic identity.

* * * *

THE EXPERTS WHO MISSED PALM SUNDAY

Scripture Lesson: Luke 19:29–40

Most of us have a love/hate feeling about experts. We seek them out when we need highly qualified and specialized help; when we're dealing with issues of medicine, financial counsel, or legal advice, we want someone who knows everything there is to know. But the rest of the time we like to poke fun at experts. "Experts," we say. "What do they know?" Or we resort to one of the standard mocking definitions: "An expert is an ordinary person a hundred miles from home" or "Expert? X is an unknown quantity, and *spurt* is hot air under pressure."

In truth, we have reason to be ambivalent about experts, because experts sometimes miss the point even in the very area of their expertise. Sometimes they miss it badly. And that probably figures, because the more expert we become, the more we isolate ourselves from opinions outside the box, and the more confident we become in our own wisdom. It was an expert, Thomas A. Edison, who said that moving pictures—one of Edison's own inventions—would never amount to anything. Yet every year, roughly a billion people watch the annual festival of the moving-picture industry, the Academy Awards ceremony. Lee DeForest, whose invention of the audio tube made radio and television possible, was surely an expert. But of the potential for television, DeForest said, "While theoretically and technically television may be feasible, commercially and financially I consider it an impossibility, a development of which we need waste little time dreaming."[1] Or if you prefer an example at a more popular level, think of Jim Denny, manager of the Grand Ole Opry and therefore a bona fide expert on matters of entertainment. He fired Elvis Presley after one performance, telling the young singer, "If I were you, I'd go back to driving a truck."[2]

And that's the way it was nearly two thousand years ago. A young teacher had come out of Nazareth. He was a great storyteller, with stories that often shocked his listeners with their quiet, powerful points. He was a compassionate man who healed the sick and paid attention to marginal people. Before long, crowds followed him everywhere he appeared. Some in these crowds began to whisper that perhaps this was the messiah, the one of whom the ancient prophets had spoken and for whom the nation had prayed and waited so long.

So the experts came to take a look. In that time and place, the experts who mattered most were not politicians or economists or scientists but theologians. The Jews were a religious people. They believed that the future of their nation was wrapped up with the purposes of God. So the experts they cared about were their religious experts, the persons best trained in the ways of God. And they had some good ones—people who spent their time and phenomenal energy seeking to comprehend the law of God and to fulfill it. The best of these were the scribes and Pharisees. I doubt that any of us has known someone who pursued religious knowledge with the intensity that marked these persons.

So it stands to reason that if anyone would recognize the messiah when he came, it would be some of these people. These people who knew the most were generally turned off by Jesus. I won't try to analyze the reasons; some had to do with professional jealousy, others with the town from which Jesus came (Nazareth was not in the mainstream of achievement), and still others with their personal prejudices as to what sort of person the messiah should be. The issue reached its peak the day we now call Palm Sunday. Jesus came to the capital, Jerusalem, the city of God and the center of every Jewish dream, and made a symbolic entrance into the city. He rode a young donkey, one never ridden before. The Hebrew prophet Zechariah had said that their great future king would make just such an entrance, "triumphant and victorious," riding on "a colt, the foal of a donkey" (Zechariah 9:9). It was as if Jesus were declaring, "I'm the one. Now what are you going to do about it?"

Some people knew what to do. A crowd began to gather; Luke calls it a "whole multitude" (Luke 19:37). They began to shout as loudly as they could, praising God for the miracles they had seen. "Blessed is the king," they cried, "who comes in the name of the Lord! Peace in heaven, and glory in the highest heaven!" (Luke 19:37–38).

But the people who declared their faith in Jesus that day were not the experts. They were fishermen and farmers, tax collectors and prostitutes, little children and homemakers. There wasn't a real expert in the crowd. We learn later that two experts—one named Nicodemus and the other Joseph of Arimathea—recognized who Jesus was, but they were afraid to declare their position. Besides, we don't know if they were even present on this particular day. The experts who were there, some Pharisees, told Jesus to keep the crowd quiet. Jesus answered, "I tell you, if these were silent, the stones would shout out" (Luke 19:40). That is, someone must acknowledge what is happening today. If the experts won't do so, the common people will. And if they don't, God will become still more common, and will give a voice to the stones of the field. One way or another, a word must be spoken today, and it will be.

But as for the experts, they missed Palm Sunday. The Messiah came, and the very people who ought to have recognized him and who should have been in the front row of acclamation were on the edge of the crowd, criticizing.

How did it happen? How is it that the experts missed Jesus?

Generally speaking, experts look for the predictable. They've been trained all through their careers to know the usual boundaries. You don't often find contrarians among the experts. Experts can list case histories, statistical studies, and polling results. They know by their studies which candidates will win, which soup or cereal will sell in which market, and which athlete should be taken first in the draft. They can spread charts across half an auditorium to prove their conclusions. And generally their conclusions are within the safe boundaries of the way things have been in the past.

So perhaps we can't blame the experts for missing Jesus. His résumé wasn't that impressive. His father, to the best of people's knowledge, was a carpenter, probably a kind of village handyman. Jesus came from a small town, Nazareth, a town with no reputation for producing leaders. As for his education, he wasn't what you would call an Ivy League product; no one knew for sure where he'd gotten his training, except that it had come through some of the local rabbis in Nazareth. You didn't expect top-drawer rabbis in Nazareth. Therefore, by the usual standards of evaluation, Jesus didn't have much of an education. As a matter of fact, no one had really heard of him until fairly recently. From what they knew, he had been working in a carpenter's shop, trying to support his widowed mother. His brief public career was hardly enough to suggest lasting prominence.

So what do we say of these experts who missed Jesus? We have to concede that Jesus didn't fit their profile. Perhaps if they had put aside some of their particular intellectual and social prejudices, they would have seen many reasons to apply the prophecies of the Hebrew Scriptures to Jesus. But they had already worked out some definitions that ruled out Jesus.

And of course, these ancient scholars should have reminded themselves that God doesn't necessarily do things our way. If there's any clear message through all the Scriptures, it is that God's ways don't necessarily coincide with our expectations. God, being God, has the right to do things in whatever way fits the divine plan. And human as we are, we somehow never fully grasp this fact, even though we may concede that it is so. When God was choosing a father for the Jewish people, the chosen one was not the firstborn son of Isaac and Rebekah but the second son, Jacob. When Israel badly needed a new king, God didn't choose someone in the traditional ranks of power; instead, there was a journey to a farm family near Bethlehem, where the youngest and least likely son, a shepherd boy named David, was chosen. And when it was time for God's special invasion of our planet, the center of action was not the then-world capital, Rome, nor the intellectual capital, Athens, nor the spiritual capital, Jerusalem, but a one-road village, Bethlehem.

The scribes and Pharisees knew the history of their people better than anyone, so they were in the best of positions to know that God's ways are not necessarily our ways. But somehow what makes perfect sense as history is off the chart as current events.

Come to think of it, even the crowds who applauded Jesus on Palm Sunday got only part of the story. It's clear they expected Jesus was now on the fast track to the kingdom. When they threw their coats and palm branches in his path, it was not to smooth the way to Golgotha; they were aiming for a throne room. They could not have imagined that by Friday afternoon their master would be hanging on a cross. I suspect we still have something of the same problem. If we had our way, we would go directly from Palm Sunday, with its acclaim, to Easter, with its ultimate triumph. We would gladly skip this week in the church calendar called Passion Week, the week that commemorates the suffering and death of our Lord.

No wonder, then, that it was hard for the first-century experts to predict God's choices and plans. Peggy Noonan, speechwriter for President Ronald Reagan, and frequent contributor to the *Wall Street Journal*, says, "The way I see it, life isn't flat and thin and 'realistic,' it's rich and full of mystery and surprise." For that reason, Peggy says that she watches the tabloid press, because she has a feeling that if God were to do something quite out of the ordinary, the mainstream press would ignore it, but it would be reported in those checkout-counter tabloids.[3]

I'm not quite ready to follow Peggy Noonan to the tabloid rack, but I know what she's saying. If I may dare, I think she's saying what I'm trying just now to say: that the experts sometimes miss the most important stories, the most eternity-shaping facts, precisely because they're experts.

I am deeply, gladly convinced that God is at work in our world. I don't believe God has forsaken our planet, though we've surely given reason for God do so. But I'm fearful that I might miss God, and that the church might miss God. I preach in some twenty-five or more churches each year, usually for a weekend—long enough to see some of the best of what a church is doing. Sometimes between worship services or while waiting for a lecture setting, I stand and wonder: If the Lord were to come to this church, would they recognize him? Would they be able to get past their church business—their youth event, their women's meeting, their men's bowling league—to see Jesus if he came, riding his donkey? Or would we be so busy talking our pleasant club talk (nothing bad, mind you, but nothing very redemptive either) that we wouldn't even notice the Lord of glory going by?

And I worry about me. I hasten to note that I'm only a second-rate expert. I wouldn't qualify as a scribe or a Pharisee. But I've been a church professional for more years than you can imagine, stretching back to my late teens. That's why I might miss God. When this year's Palm Sunday procession occurs, I could easily be one of those Pharisees standing at the edge of the crowd, critiquing the whole event.

You see, there *are* some Palm Sunday processionals going on today. God is, indeed, still entering our world; not on a physical donkey, as our Lord did nearly twenty centuries ago, but just as surely and just as wonderfully and just as unpredictably. I want to be "in" on such an event. I want to be one of those who cheers God on! And that's what I want for you, too.

But we'll miss God's big events if we decide beforehand that we know how God has to do it. And we'll miss it unless we're humble enough to receive it—humble enough, that is, to stand by the roadside of our world and cheer for heaven, cheer for a Lord who, to our surprise, sometimes chooses to make his entrance riding a donkey.

NOTES

1. Stephen Danadio, Joan Smith, Susan Mesner, and Rebecca Davison, eds., *The New York Public Library Book of Twentieth Century American Quotations* (New York: Warner Books, 1992), 334.
2. Albert Goldman, *Elvis* (New York: McGraw-Hill Book Co., 1981), 122.
3. Peggy Noonan, *What I Saw at the Revolution* (New York: Random House, 1990), 32.

6

Holy Week Noontime Services

As surely as there is a time and a tide in the affairs of human creatures, so there is in programming and activities of the church. A generation ago, most major cities and a good number of smaller cities and communities brought the celebration of the Lenten season to a climax by a series of noonday services during Holy Week, usually in a downtown church and almost always under cooperative church sponsorship. In many communities these services were the most visible and effective of ecumenical events, bringing to those communities as guest speakers a wide variety of the best-known preachers of the time.

But demographics change, and people's enthusiasms ebb and flow. At present, not many cities have such a Holy Week series, though a few remain. But this doesn't mean that the basic structure has been completely discarded. In some smaller cities and towns, several congregations combine for Holy Week services on Sunday through Wednesday evenings. In far more instances, individual congregations are finding that Holy Week is an ideal time for a call to deeper commitment. In such instances, churches often have preaching services Sunday through Wednesday evenings, then conclude the emphasis with a Communion service on Maundy Thursday. A pastor is wise to build the program around the capacity and interests of his or her people. Some find that participation improves when a meal is served prior to the services. This is especially true in suburban churches, where persons may come directly from work to join their families in the church dining room.

As for the time and tide, who knows what may develop in the next decade? The downtown ecumenical service may again come into its own. There's really no sure way to predict how our tastes and interests will change.

The person who preaches in services of this kind ought to begin with the conviction that those who attend are particularly in earnest. They may not appear so to the casual eye. Some may come simply because they come to everything the church offers—and such loyalty, whatever its source, is not to be despised. But in almost every instance, the people who come to special Holy Week events are true seekers; they feel something of the solemnity of the season, and they want, however incoherently, to find a deeper place in God.

I have preached this sermon, in slightly varied forms, in several settings. The first time was in a union noonday Holy Week service held at the Old Stone Church in Cleveland, Ohio. The second time was at a service in downtown Houston, Texas, at the First United Methodist Church. The most recent was part of a Holy Week emphasis at Bryan College in Dayton, Tennessee. The age and geographical variety in these events was great, but the response was in all instances remarkably receptive.

* * * *

WHAT CAN BE SAID FOR TUESDAYS?

Scripture Lesson: Ecclesiastes 3:1–8

So it's Tuesday, and what can be said for Tuesday? A wise writer long ago said that for everything there is a season, and a time for every matter under heaven, so we have to judge that Tuesday has its place. But in the general run of our days, Tuesdays seem to have a poor, forgotten share. Sunday is so wondrous that John Newton called it "Day of all the week, the best."[1] Monday has a kind of negative grandeur, as the back-to-work, back-to-school day, a resumption of normal order. Wednesday marks the midweek and for that reason gets a good share of special meetings. Friday has gotten its unique four-letter identity: TGIF —"Thank God it's Friday." As for Saturday, it's the day of worship for some, of shopping for many, and party night for still others.

But what can be said for Tuesday? What significance can we give to Tuesday?

Now it's Tuesday of Holy Week, and the same rule seems to hold. Holy Week began with what we now call Palm Sunday, or Passion Sunday. Monday is generally seen as the day when Jesus drove the money changers from the Temple. Wednesday is considered the day Judas Iscariot went to the chief priests to arrange the betrayal of our Lord, and Thursday was the day the Lord's Supper was instituted, the day we now refer to as Maundy Thursday. And of course Friday is the day we now call Good Friday; no one needs to defend its glory. But what about *Tuesday*?

Some Bible scholars say that the Tuesday of Holy Week was a day of teaching, in which the Pharisees tried to entrap Jesus. Others, however, call it Silent Tuesday because they find no sure evidence that anything special happened on that day. So what shall we say about the Tuesday of Holy Week? I dare to say that Holy Week is the most significant single week of all human history; is there any significance to the Tuesday of that week?

I want us to find the weight of this day, because I sense it might carry a lesson for us all. We have a hint of the issue in this, that on the day we now call Palm Sunday, crowds in the

city of Jerusalem hailed Jesus as a public hero. He was the one
for whom they had waited, on whom their nation's hopes
rested. But less than five days later, the crowds called for Jesus
to be crucified.

Something must have happened between Sunday and Friday.
What turned an adoring throng into a bloodthirsty mob, or at
the least into silent, noncommittal bystanders? What peculiar
chemistry changed the "Hosannas" into "Crucify him"?

"Crowds are like that," someone answers. "It's just another
instance of mob psychology." But that doesn't answer the question; it only gives us a name for the action. When, in less than
five days, did the weight of the scale shift from adulation to
hatred? What happened on Monday, or Tuesday, or Wednesday that set up Thursday night and Friday morning?

That is, what is the weight of a single day? Somewhere in the
course of that week, the balance shifted. On Sunday, the enemies of Jesus were afraid because the crowds were so rapt; by
Friday, those enemies were simply the lead voices in a cre-
scendo of destruction. What was the weight of a day, during
that crucial week, that turned it all?

I remember a professor who reminded us once of the way in
which a single day, a single insignificant decision, can turn life
to a new course. He put it this way: "Suppose, today, as you
leave this classroom, you go out the front door of the building
rather than your usual pattern through the back way to the dor-
mitories. And suppose, just as you go out, you come upon
someone you've never met, and the conversation changes the
whole direction of your life?" As we pondered the possibility,
but the unlikelihood, of such a turn, he shared his own story—
the story that made him raise such a hypothetical question.
Years before, during the Great Depression, he was running to
catch a city bus. He was just out of high school and wanted terribly to go to college but had no money, so he was going downtown to apply for a job. Now he had missed the bus and was
likely to be late for his appointment. When he boarded the next
bus, he took the first empty seat, beside a man he didn't know.
They struck up a conversation. Before the bus ride ended, the
stranger had worked out a way for my professor to go to col-

lege. Everything in his life and career was changed, it seems, by his missing one bus and catching another.

You've heard stories like that. If you're sentimental, you may have one of your own, with touches of romance. But of course, there's more to such a story than just a chance meeting. There is the element of *decision*. My teacher's story emphasized the element of chance, but there's still a choice, or choices, to be made after chance has happened. If I meet some special individual, what will I do with the meeting? If I receive some offer, what answer will I give? I think of a man on that first Good Friday, Simon of Cyrene. There was never a person more surely caught by chance than that man. He had come to Jerusalem, we may suppose, to celebrate the festival of the Passover, and while standing in the crowded streets, he was apprehended to pick up the cross under which Jesus had stumbled. The soldiers might have grabbed any one of the dozen, twenty, or thirty people in close reach. Or for that matter, Jesus might have fallen five steps earlier or later, eliminating Simon from consideration. But by chance, the lot fell on Simon.

Yet how Simon responded to that event was not chance but choice. He might, you know, have burned with such resentment as to miss entirely the wonder of encountering Christ. A little of "Why me?" or "It's not fair!" or "What rotten luck!" and the occasion would have had no significant sequel. It seems, however, that Simon responded rightly, because it seems that his sons, Alexander and Rufus, became leaders in the early Christian church. Whatever fortune caused the hand to be laid on Simon, it was Simon's use of that fortune that made all the difference.

In the end, the decision of Holy Week was not a mob decision but the decisions of individuals. It's easy to excuse ourselves, by proxy, when we read the story of Holy Week. We think of the crowd that cursed our Lord on Good Friday, but ultimately, there is no such thing as a crowd; there are only individuals. Multitudes from Hitler's Germany said later that they bore no responsibility for the atrocities performed on the Jews; they saw themselves as helpless individuals who had been swept along by the tide of the masses, with no real decision on their part.

Not so. A mob or a crowd is always made up of individuals. Those individuals decide, one by one, whether they will crucify with the mob or whether they will stand erect for goodness. In the world of Nazi Germany there was still a Corrie ten Boom, and Dietrich Bonhoeffer, and Martin Niemoeller, and hundreds of others whose names are lost to us but who dared to vote contrary to the mob. The mob may influence us, may shout us down and threaten us. They may even win. But they can't cast our vote. That vote is made deep in the quiet of the soul, and ultimately, no one is responsible but the one who makes it.

So what happened between Palm Sunday and Good Friday? Take one person out of that crowd, any single one, and follow that person. Imagine yourself to be that person. What was the weight of a day in that week? Of Tuesday, perhaps?

I said earlier that, according to tradition, Tuesday may have been a day of teaching, in which Jesus was challenged by his enemies. Is it possible that Jesus' teachings became too demanding that Tuesday? Certainly, he cut the line sharply during Holy Week—the cleansing of the Temple, for instance. Did some say, on the day after the cleansing, "Count me out. I thought he was going to be a healer and a teacher, but he's nothing but a troublemaker. Count me out"?

Or did some of those people—people like you and me—begin on Tuesday to reevaluate the cost? Did they sense the tide was turning? This could have been especially the case as Jesus offered his incisive teachings regarding judgment. I wonder if some hearers, erstwhile disciples, began to sense the meaning of discipleship. During my years as a pastor, I was saddened often to find that persons who had joined the church were offended when something was expected of their joining. When asked for a pledge of money or for attendance at worship or for disciplined Christian living, they resented it. I remember someone saying, "I thought I'd find love in the church!" They seemed not to relate love to responsibility. Perhaps in that first Holy Week some wandered away on Tuesday as they contemplated the price tag on the good news.

Or consider the other tradition, that this was Silent Tuesday, a day in which nothing special happened. So many of us fade away on life's silent days. So often our best resolves are destroyed not by violent opposition but by ennui or a slow sapping of our intentions; indeed, sometimes just by the passing of time itself, and the competing absorptions that come with passing time. One evening more than forty years ago, when I was a student in graduate school, someone raised a playful philosophical question as we whiled away a pleasant evening of conversation: If a fire should break out in the apartment building where we lived, what one item—other than a human life, of course—would we try to save from our lodgings?

It was a no-brainer for me. Without hesitation I pointed to a large box of research notes. "That box," I said. "It represents so much work, so many hundreds of hours of my life." Well, the years have gone by and no fire has destroyed that valued box. But time has—time and neglect. The collection that I would have saved that night, above all else, lies useless on a shelf in our garage, destroyed by neglect. Perhaps it was so with some in the crowd from Palm Sunday: those people who didn't turn against Jesus or become disenchanted with him but who just became absorbed in the common business of the week. More souls are lost, I'm quite sure, by the silent Tuesdays of life—the sheer daily minutiae of living—than by any grand crisis. You don't need to be part of a crowd that screams, "Crucify him!" You need only absent yourself from the issues and become so involved in other things that you don't even realize a showdown has come.

So now it is Tuesday again, and once more the drama of the ages is playing. There is not the grand excitement of Palm Sunday, nor is there the awesome, ugly showdown of Good Friday. It is an ordinary day. What could be more ordinary than a Tuesday? It's a day of sunshine, honking horns, errands to be run, phone calls to be answered, e-mail to be attended to.

And ordinary days are the ones to be watched. We rise to the crises of life, but watch out for the Tuesdays! They catch us off guard because their profiles are so commonplace, so unthreatening.

So guard this Tuesday well. It is a holy day—not simply because it is part of Holy Week but because every week is holy and because every day is a potential day of decision. Every day our souls go to the eternal ballot box. Consider the massive weight of this day, how in it you and I may shift the balance to good or evil—for ourselves, for our families, for our cities and our country, for our world. So give this day to God, with gladness and with a holy passion. Because believe me, if we do right by our Tuesdays, our common days, our forgettable days, we will be true to our Lord in the crises named Friday.

NOTES

1. John Newton, "Safely through Another Week," in *The Methodist Hymnal* (Nashville: The Methodist Publishing House, 1966), #489.

7

Easter Sunday

For several years of my ministry I had in my congregation a remarkable couple, Clifford and Florence Northcott. He was a retired bishop of the United Methodist Church; indeed, the bishop who had presided at my ordination. One day during Holy Week, he stopped in my office to inquire about my welfare. Then he spoke words that were half wistful and half admonitory. Recalling his own years as a pastor, he said, "Easter Sunday so often left me feeling defeated. It was the Sunday with the largest attendance of the year, and the finest opportunity to reach the unchurched or the marginal. But the week preceding was always the most hectic—taking Communion to shut-ins, extra services on Maundy Thursday and Good Friday, unexpected visitors. As a result, on the Sunday when my preaching should have been the best, I was often the most poorly prepared."

Most pastors know the feeling. Part of the problem can be solved by better planning. Unfortunately, since Easter comes only once a year, it's hard to carry the good resolves and wisdom from one Easter to the next.

But time is not the preacher's only enemy as Easter approaches. Sameness is the other, and it may be an even greater hazard than time. The parish pastor wonders how to tell the Easter story in such a way that it will really, truly be heard. Most of the people who sit in the pews on Easter Sunday, including especially those for whom church is a decidedly infrequent experience, have a great collection of superficial impressions about Easter. The preacher has to get past this montage of spring flowers, bunnies, and Easter eggs and declare the extraordinary good news of Easter. And in truth, many who come aren't really hungry for that kind of content. They're happier with the commonplaces of sentiment than the substance of truth. No matter; we should aim for substance. But make sure the substance is warm and winsome.

I hardly need to offer background information about Easter; you know all that could be given in a brief statement. But I urge you to spend some time reviewing the Orthodox tradition, particularly in its ethnic varieties. Such a visit to the unfamiliar may give you a creative vantage point for the familiar.

The sermon that follows was preached at the Church of the Saviour in Cleveland, Ohio, on Easter Sunday, 1988. It was the sixteenth Easter sermon I had preached in that church. One of the ways I helped myself keep freshness in my Easter sermons was by making the Easter sermon part of a Lenten series. Thus, while dealing with familiar themes, I did so through the lens of particular overarching themes. For instance, an Easter sermon during a series on the Lord's Prayer had the title "The Shout of Triumph" ("For thine is the kingdom, and the power, and the glory, forever," suggesting that the early church added these words to the prayer because the resurrection of their Lord made it impossible to end the prayer otherwise); and for a series on Psalm 23, "Goodness and Mercy Follow Me."

In the instance of the sermon that follows, I was in the concluding months of my long pastorate at this church. My Lenten series had carried the general title "Some Things I Have Learned." So for Easter Sunday I chose "What I Have Learned about Life." As you will see, the Easter message is set in the context of one person's lifetime (so far!) of learning.

* * * *

What I Have Learned about Life

Scripture Lesson: John 11:17–27

If you're the sort of person who comes to church only—or primarily—on Christmas Eve and Easter, I should tell you something. I love Christmas, but I love Easter more. Christmas is wonderful, because it says so much about giving and loving, both on God's part and on ours, and because it is wrapped in such warm and lovely layers of sentiment. But Easter is magnificent, because it tells me that I am destined, by the grace of God, to *win*. It doesn't tell me the exact score in this game of life, but it does tell me that I'm on the winning side, and that there's no doubt about it.

I know quite a bit about death. I've come to that Jordan River often, as a person and as a pastor, and have cast a wistful eye to the other side. I still remember the first time I saw a person die. He was someone I'd never met. I was called to the hospital because the man's own pastor was out of town. As it happened, I was the only one in the room when the last breath came. I can still remember the slight shudder in his body. I stepped out of the room to talk with the man's wife. "How old was your husband?" I asked, trying to falter my way into some kind of conversation. "Twenty-nine," she said. I was startled, as if I'd been hit, because I was then twenty-nine. I felt, like John Donne, that this man's death had diminished me, because no one, it seemed to me then, died at my age.

I have seen the insistent range of death. Some in old age have asked me to pray that they might die, to be with those they loved the most. Some in intense suffering have put me in awe by their courage and peace as they have looked for weeks into the very face of death. And sometimes I have dealt with death when everything right and logical said that death had no right to come so early.

Some of those deaths have made me wish I weren't a preacher, because at such times a pastor is expected to fill a place no human is sufficient to fill. I have tried to be the intermediary between death and life at services for infants who died within hours of birth, and for children struck down by accident or disease, and for young people just at the threshold of their dreams. I confess that I could not conduct such funeral or memorial services if I did not believe there is a promised land on the other side of the Jordan River.

Twice my experience with death has come within the close bonds of family. I'm fortunate that it is only twice. I finished a speech one time, years ago, in Milwaukee, and as I left the platform a preacher-friend took my arm. "I have some bad news for you, Ellsworth," he said. A long-distance call had come during the speech; my mother had died, quite without warning. I remember standing alone in a room of the funeral parlor two days later, looking at the body of my mother. Suddenly I understood, as never before, that the veil between this world and the next is tissue-thin. Indeed, in that moment I felt closer to my mother than at any time when she was alive. The apostle Paul had a word for it: "For now we see through a glass, darkly; but then face to face" (1 Corinthians 13:12, KJV). I realized our closeness at that moment because on *her* side, though not yet on mine, the veil was down. She had crossed the river to a place of perfect understanding; and by faith, I could see her on that better side.

Then, some years later, I received a call sometime between Saturday night and Sunday morning. My father had died. Somehow the death of a second parent is different. The roots that tie us to the past are torn up. There is now no home to which one can return. I remember awakening my daughter, then nine years old, to tell her that her grandpa was dead and that now she was my special blood tie, my continuity in life. I'm sure it was beyond the comprehension of a half-sleeping nine-year-old, even a very sensitive one, but I had to say it. In a sense, I was talking to myself. But when I traveled back to the church my parents had loved and supported and heard the familiar words of faith and hope and profound assurance, I knew—surely and beyond doubt—that my father had crossed his Jordan River. He had gone over into the promised land.

Such feelings well up in the soul insistently because of Easter. That's why I look forward so much to every Easter Sunday. I believe in "the life everlasting" all through the year, but my soul wants a special day when I can throw my hands into the air and shout it. "He is risen!" my heart cries, and I'm glad for this Sunday when that grand exclamation is part of the ritual of the day.

That's part of what I have learned about life in the decades of following Jesus Christ. But important as that is, it's only a small part of what I've learned. Because as I perceive it, Easter applies not only to that moment when, at the junction of death, we bid farewell to someone we love, nor at that other moment when we ourselves cross over to the world to come. I see Easter as a continuing fact of life right here, right now, every day.

Consider our Scripture lesson of the morning. There was a family in the little village of Bethany who loved Jesus dearly. They were two sisters and a brother, all single—Mary, Martha, and Lazarus. One day, death invaded their home without warning, taking Lazarus. When Jesus came, four days later, Martha said to him, "Lord, if you had been here, my brother would not have died." That's how simply and fully she believed in Jesus' power.

In his reply to Martha, Jesus said, "I am the resurrection and the life. Those who believe in me, even though they die, will live, and everyone who lives and believes in me will never die" (John 11:25–26). A whole principle of life and resurrection begins to operate in us when we take Jesus Christ as Lord of life. And it is present tense. Jesus did not announce that he would, at some later time, be the source of life; "I *am*," he said. Always and ever, even now, Jesus Christ is eternal life.

One of the early Christian documents, the First Epistle of John, puts it directly and uncompromisingly: "And this is the testimony: God gave us eternal life, and this life is in his Son. Whoever has the Son has life" (1 John 5:11–12). This life of which I speak is not something I'm hoping to collect on when I die; it is mine already. Easter began for me and in me those many years ago, when I accepted Jesus Christ as Lord of my life. I note that phrase: "Lord of my *life*." The very word takes on new dimensions when Christ becomes its Lord.

My late friend Nate Thorp used to quote a brother-in-law who said that most people "die and then grow old." How true!

That's what I have in mind when I speak of the Easter principle, and when I try to tell you what I have learned about life. We live in a world where so many people die while they're still walking about. Some show it dramatically by becoming consumed with alcohol and other drugs. Others run about frenetically, as if by their running they might deny that death has set in. And still others show it by the resignation with which they live.

Now, let me hasten to confess that death is a strong and clamorous voice. It constantly asserts itself, as if seeking to convince us that it is the ultimate fact of our universe. Death comes not only at that legendary last breath. It makes its claims every hour of every day, either in assaults on our own bodies or in its attacks on those we love. Death announces itself with every transient pain, every instance of poverty, every stabbing fear, every skipped beat of the heart. Death is persistent in its pursuit. It will take command of our minds unless there is some prior, stronger truth in control.

But Easter tells us that life is here, in Jesus Christ, and that it is far stronger than death. If death is insistent in its daily and hourly announcements, life is far more insistent. Sometimes that feeling about life comes dramatically, as it did a long time ago for Samuel Logan Brengle. Two days after his conversion, Brengle wrote of his feelings as he walked over Boston Common before breakfast. His happiness was so complete that he was weeping for uncluttered joy. "Oh, how I love!" he wrote. "In that hour I knew Jesus, and I loved Him till it seemed my heart would break with love." And with this new grasp of life, Brengle was "filled with love for all God's creatures." As the sparrows chirped, he loved them. "I saw a little worm wriggling across my path; I stepped over; I did not want to hurt any living thing. I loved the dogs, I loved the horses, I loved the little urchins on the street, I loved the strangers hurrying past me . . . I loved the whole world!"[1]

Well, no one could say that Sam Brengle had died and was now growing old! And he kept that gladness all through his life. He became a leader in the Salvation Army, legendary for his joyful, vibrant faith. What I'm trying to say is that Easter was at work in him on that morning as he walked the Boston Common, in love with the world; and in the years that followed, as he marched with the Salvation Army and prayed with derelicts.

Such a sense of new life does things to one's outlook on physical health. One of C. S. Lewis's closest friends, a man called Shelburne, wrote Lewis a somewhat doleful report about his earaches, his toothaches, and the possibility of an operation. Lewis replied, "We must both, I'm afraid, recognize that, as we grow older, we become like old cars—more and more repairs and replacements are necessary. We must look forward to the fine new machines (latest resurrection model) which are waiting for us, we hope, in the Divine Garage."[2] The pains of our bodies are put in perspective if we know a new body awaits us up the road.

I feel that way about life as a whole, and about every detail of its makeup. This is because I see the beautiful fallout of the resurrection in all of life. I think of an occasion when I was approaching an out-of-state preaching engagement. Somehow a major detail had been bungled. It promised inconvenience and confusion, the sort of thing likely to upset someone of my temperament. But I really and quite simply believed that God would bring good from it. Whatever had caused the mishap, whether a lapse of memory on my part or a failure of a person on the other end, was ultimately inconsequential. What mattered was that God is at work in our world, so that all the little deaths in our world—and the medium-sized and big deaths, too—are turned into life, when we allow ourselves to be part of a resurrection faith.

Day by day, therefore, I expect to claim the resurrection. In every circumstance of life, every frustration and commonplace, every picayunish detail, I expect resurrection. That's part of what Easter means to me—right here, right now. That's part of what I have learned about life, because of Easter.

Arthur Gordon tells of a wonderful older woman in Georgia who has lived her life with enormous energy and accomplishment. When Gordon asked her the secret, she smiled and said it was something she had learned from her grandmother before her. It was summed up in just nine words: *Love life, and it will love you right back.*[3]

I believe our universe is made that way. I believe God made us for life, and made life for us, and if we will love life, it will embrace us even as we embrace it. However, if we draw back from life, become fearful of it, dread it, it begins to defeat us. Life, ironically and perversely, ceases to be our ally.

The best way I know to fall in love with life is to find the new life that is in Jesus Christ. It is not a way of life that guarantees exemption from troubles, disappointment, sickness, and such. But it is a life that is so strong, so full of resurrection power, that it turns all the stuff of life, good and bad, into victory.

That's why I'm singing this Easter morning. I believe in the resurrection of our Lord Jesus Christ, and in life eternal. And I believe that this new life in Christ is already at work in our world, even now. Whatever happens, therefore, I believe that *Life* will win. There can be no loss, ultimately, since Jesus Christ is Lord of life. I believe this is what Jesus was saying to Martha so long ago—not only about the restoration of her brother but about the whole principle of each day. I believe in life now, and I believe in it for the world to come.

That's what I've learned, so far, about life. Thanks be to God! Christ is risen. He is risen, indeed.

NOTES

1. Quoted in Emile Cailliet, *Journey into Light* (Grand Rapids: Zondervan, 1968), 107–8.
2. William Griffin, *Clive Staples Lewis: A Dramatic Life* (San Francisco: Harper & Row, 1986), 398.
3. Arthur Gordon, *A Touch of Wonder* (Carmel, N.Y.: Guideposts Associates, 1974), 106.

8

Low Sunday

(The Second Sunday of Easter)

Some preachers think that Low Sunday is only a joke; what better name could you give the Sunday after Easter, they reason, the Sunday that seems like nothing but a letdown after the exhilaration of Easter? In my pastoral days, I would often have one or more visiting clergy in my church on the Sunday after Easter, on vacation from their own pulpit and often asking why I was preaching; why not an associate pastor or a guest speaker?

But Low Sunday exists, even if its name is probably a mistake. Here's the story, as best we know it. The names that were popularly given to certain Sundays and other holy days were sometimes the product of misunderstanding. After all, only a few persons understood the Latin of the mass, so some features of the mass became, for most people, what they thought they were hearing. The mass for the Sunday after Easter included frequent use of the Latin word for "praise," *laudo*. It seems that some heard this word as "low," and since it appeared so often in that mass, they began referring to the day as "low Sunday."

Circumstances have contrived with the misunderstanding, particularly in Protestant churches, and in Catholic churches too since faithful attendance has ceased to be as rigorously encouraged. So clergy are quick to consider the name descriptive of attendance: Low Sunday indeed, by way of comparison with the Easter services just a week earlier!

Laurence Hull Stookey recommends, in his excellent book on the church calendar, that the Low Sunday designation "be abandoned in favor of a title that has clear meaning."[1] I decided instead to make the most of a questionable situation when I was asked to preach at the Aldersgate United Methodist Church in Nixa, Missouri, on the Sunday following Easter in 2003. The name and its place in the calendar seemed to me to have too many homiletical possibilities to be passed by.

The point, specifically, is this: The church calendar identifies the series of Sundays beginning with Easter as the seven Sundays of Easter, and I suspect that for most churchgoers, and probably for a good share of clergy, the days have no applied significance beyond the numbering. "Low Sunday" gave me a chance to extend the Easter message. I encourage you, whether by Low Sunday or another of the Sundays of Easter, to do the same.

* * * *

EASTER ISN'T OVER

Scripture Lesson: John 20:19–28

I don't have to tell you that last Sunday was Easter Sunday, nor that the Sunday before that was Palm Sunday, or Passion Sunday; all of you know that. And if you're more carefully tuned to the church calendar, you also know that in six weeks we'll celebrate Pentecost Sunday. But I'm quite certain that not many of you here know what today is; and if you do, it's probably because you've heard some joke about the name that's been given to this day.

Today is *Low Sunday*. Low, as in l-o-w; low, as in "down"; low, as in "not high." Low Sunday.

This is the accepted religious name in the English-speaking world for this Sunday, at least for the past several hundred years. No one is entirely sure why. The title may come from the days when worship in the Catholic Church was in Latin. The Latin word for praise, *laudo*, was prominent in the worship on the Sunday after Easter, and it's possible the priests and the well educated called this Sunday *Laudo* Sunday. The uneducated, who were a decided majority in those centuries, may have understood this as Low Sunday; so, in time, the "Low Sunday" title stuck.

As you might guess, the title has taken on a life of its own among clergy. The drop in attendance between Easter Sunday and the Sunday after Easter has made the name a matter of humor in the profession: "Low Sunday, indeed! The attendance shows it."

Personally, I think the name has something to commend it. Not in regard to attendance: from my own pastoral experience, I concluded that attendance on the Sunday after Easter was, in truth, generally somewhat better than the average—perhaps because many folks who came on Easter got just enough religion to try still another Sunday! The reason the Sunday after Easter has gotten such a bad rap for attendance is because it looks so bad by comparison.

But the title "Low Sunday" has significance. It may have come by way of errors in hearing or pronunciation, but the word fits. You realize as much when you look somewhat carefully at what the New Testament says about the days—indeed, the weeks—following the first Easter. This was not a period of exuberance, as you and I reason that it ought to have been. Those first Christians, the people who had the most intimate experience with Easter, had a difficult time getting hold of the resurrection story. We have an edge on them, you know. Our modern celebration of Easter may leave a good deal to be desired, but those of us who truly believe know that Easter recalls the magnificent victory over the power of death. As Saint Paul put it, "Where, O death, is your victory? Where, O death, is your sting?" (1 Cor. 15:55). Death has been defeated by our Lord's triumph at Easter. I'm quite sure that not many modern churchgoers fully realize the magnitude of this victory, but nevertheless we get some of the blessed fallout on Easter. The music, the flowers, the special efforts to dress up—all these things give a wonderful exuberance to the day, and even if many Christians don't fully grasp the Easter story, they can't help but feel something of its wonder and beauty.

But it wasn't that simple for the first followers of Jesus. On the days after the first Easter there was a great deal that could be called *low*: low feelings, low spirits, low expectations; indeed, shattered expectations.

Consider the story in our Scripture lesson of the day. A number of Jesus' followers had experienced Easter in some form or other only hours earlier. Some had seen the empty tomb, and Mary Magdalene had actually seen Jesus and had talked with him at the tomb. Others had seen Jesus as the day had unfolded. You'd think, therefore, that they would be on top of the world; their Lord had been crucified and had even been placed in a tomb, but behold, the power of the tomb had been broken, and he was alive! Jesus was wonderfully, gloriously alive!

But that isn't the way those early believers saw it. On the evening of that first Easter, according to the Gospel writer, the believers were in a house where the doors were locked. They had shut themselves away, because they were afraid of what would happen next; afraid of their enemies, of the people who had apprehended and crucified Jesus. They weren't holding a resurrection party—or if they were, it was an exceedingly quiet one. They were simply seeking a way to keep out of sight, to keep alive. Now you and I, from this distance, might consider their fears ridiculous. After all, if God had raised Jesus from the dead, God could certainly take care of their enemies. But that isn't the way they felt. Easter had happened only a dozen or fifteen hours earlier, but for the followers of Jesus, it was a *low* time.

One of the apostles, Thomas, wasn't there that evening. When the others told him that Jesus had visited them, Thomas didn't express regret that he had missed the landmark occasion; instead, he scorned their story. Our postmodern, scientific world sometimes thinks ours is the first generation ever to look at matters skeptically. Not so! Those first generation believers were as anxious for hard proof as any modern or postmodern person might be. Thomas couldn't believe there had been a resurrection. For him, this was a low day. A very low day.

And that's the way it continued for the next several weeks. Some time later, when Jesus met with the eleven disciples (Judas, you remember, was gone), we read that when the disciples saw Jesus, "they worshiped him; but *some doubted*" (Matt. 28:17). Some scholars point out that it says, literally, "they worshiped him, and they doubted," and I suspect that says it perfectly. Easter had come and gone, and they had seen Jesus a number of times in a number of places, and yet there were lingering doubts. In the midst of all the highs, there were still low moments.

Let me pause for a moment to say how grateful we should be that the Bible is a completely honest book. That's one of the many reasons you can trust it. It isn't a public relations document to sell us on a candidate, so it never skips over our human failings, or the failings of the church, or the failings of even its best heroes and heroines; it simply tells us the truth. And it tells the truth about Easter. It lets us know that after Easter, some of the people—some of our spiritual ancestors—were low. Indeed, probably all of them had low moments.

How could this be? How could they be low, when something so breathtakingly wonderful had happened? How could they doubt in the face of so much evidence? I think we should keep several factors in mind. Here's a big one: Easter wasn't what they were planning on. Jesus' disciples had been expecting an earthly kingdom, with Jesus as an all-conquering messiah. Only hours before Jesus was arrested, some of his disciples were still arguing about which of them would be greatest when Jesus assumed authority. We're always open to a very great letdown when we have mistaken expectations. Marriage is a letdown, and for some a disaster, when one or both parties discover that it isn't one long, uninterrupted honeymoon. Some young parents have second thoughts about parenthood when they discover that a baby isn't a doll or a pet you lay aside at will but a sometimes constantly demanding little prince or princess. As for some of those special events we wait for, save for, and plan for, when finally they come and are gone, we may feel like reciting the song Peggy Lee made famous: "Is That All There Is?" I'm sure the disciples found it almost impossible to adjust to the idea that Jesus wasn't going to establish a throne in Jerusalem. They had dreamed in a rather dull black and white, and they just couldn't handle Technicolor. Since their dreams were so badly askew, they were blind to the magnificent thing that had actually happened. They had been waiting for a small-time, earthly kingdom. Instead, they were eyewitnesses to the eternal victory over sin, death, and hell. And because they were looking for something so small, they couldn't seem to grasp something utterly beyond their imagination.

I'm sometimes like that, and probably you are, too. We miss some of life's greatest blessings because we've been planning on something smaller. We don't *know* that it's smaller; that's our problem. C. S. Lewis once said something to the effect that most of us are like a slum child playing in a muddy gutter who refuses a chance to go to the ocean beach because the child doesn't know such a place exists. So it is that we're often content to have a religious life that exists from one special favor or one predicament to another. We're not attracted to a disciplined walk with God that leads to profound heights and depths of living; we're ready to settle for an occasional high. God offers the wonder of a divine daily friendship, and we're disappointed because what we want (we think!) is a bellhop God who does favors for us now and then. And while looking for a God who will get us through some new predicament, we ignore the God who would be our dearest, daily, faithful friend.

But no doubt the biggest reason the first believers suffered a letdown after Easter is this: they thought Easter was the end of the story. They made Easter an event in itself, instead of a beginning. I wonder if perhaps the disciples looked upon the resurrection of Jesus as simply another miracle, like the raising of Lazarus. The raising of Lazarus was a very great and wonderful miracle, no doubt about that. But that was it; there was no more to it. The time would come when Lazarus would die again. And that might well be the way the disciples felt about the resurrection of their Lord. It was wonderful, it was inspiring—but so what? They didn't know it was the *beginning* of something that would never end. Each time Jesus appeared to them, the experience was beautiful—but they liked the old days better, when Jesus was with them all the time. Besides, in the old days they knew what to expect. They didn't know what Jesus would teach or whom he might heal, but the days were at least somewhat predictable. Now Jesus was in and out, and they didn't know when or where they might see him—and perhaps worse, they didn't know what was expected of them. No wonder, then, that they wandered about in confusion in the days after Easter, and that at one point they even thought about going back to their old careers, back to fishing.

The disciples just didn't grasp that Easter was the beginning of something utterly new and different. No wonder, then, that they had some low days after Easter.

And that's the good news I want to give you and me today: *Easter isn't over.* It didn't end last Sunday. Last Sunday was just the announcement of a new beginning.

We sometimes forget that this is what Sunday is all about. The first Christians naturally worshiped on Saturday, the seventh day, because most of them were Jews who now believed in Jesus, and they had been taught that Saturday was the right day of rest and worship. But when Easter finally got through to the early believers, they began meeting on the first day of the week, what we now call Sunday, because it was on the first day of the week that Jesus had been raised from the dead. So it is that Sunday, the day of the resurrection, became the first day of the week, the day to begin again. And that's as it should be, because Easter is the *beginning*. It's the beginning of a new life for all who will receive it.

So today may be Low Sunday on the church calendar, but it isn't low Sunday in our hearts. Rather, today is another wonderful day in the new life that Easter has brought us. It is a new day of springtime, and it would be even if we lived in the Southern Hemisphere, where this is the beginning of autumn; because the spring we know is not a matter of the calendar or of the passing seasons but of the new life that has come to our lives.

Many years ago I saw a movie. This was back in the days when movies were much simpler and slow-moving, perhaps often a little corny. And that's all right, because we were probably a little corny, too. It was a Hollywood movie about the life of Jesus. I don't know the name of it; it may have been a Cecil B. DeMille spectacular, but I can't say for sure. In those days, we knew when a movie was over because they ran a line across the screen that said, "The End." Perhaps otherwise we would have sat there and watched it over again. But when this movie on the life of Jesus came to a glorious resurrection scene, there came across the bottom of the screen a line—not "The End" but "This Was the Beginning."

The filmmaker got it right. Easter was not the end but the beginning. So I remind you this morning, whoever you are— sick or well, employed or worrying about a job, young or older, successful or feeling defeated—Easter has come, but it hasn't gone. Easter isn't over. This is only the beginning.

NOTES

1. Laurence Hull Stookey, *Calendar: Christ's Time for the Church* (Nashville: Abingdon Press, 1996), 172, n. 10.

9

Mother's Day

This American holiday has a mixed and controversial standing in the church. It could easily be argued that Mother's Day was born in the church, or at the least that the infant idea was nurtured to its strength there. Julia Ward Howe, author of "Battle Hymn of the Republic," first made a public appeal for such a day in 1872, urging that it be observed on June 2 and that it be a day dedicated to peace. A celebration was begun in Kentucky in 1887, and a campaign for such a day in Indiana in 1904, but it was a West Virginia woman, Anna Jarvis, who chose the second Sunday of May and began pushing for a nationwide observance. She persuaded churches in Philadelphia and in Grafton, West Virginia, to hold such a celebration on May 10, 1908.

But it was the 1912 General Conference of the Methodist Episcopal Church in Minneapolis that gave a platform of power to the idea by a resolution recognizing Anna Jarvis as founder of Mother's Day, with the suggestion that the second Sunday in May be the continuing time of celebration. Two years later, on May 9, 1914, President Woodrow Wilson signed a joint resolution of Congress recommending that Congress and the executive departments observe Mother's Day, and the following year Wilson was authorized to proclaim the annual observance of Mother's Day.

I suspect that many laypersons think of Mother's Day as a church holiday because it is in church that they celebrate it.

Church attendance on this day is likely to be third only to
Christmas Eve and Easter. Some worshipers still celebrate with
carnations, colored if the mother is living and white if she is
deceased. Attention is sometimes paid to the oldest mother, the
youngest mother, and particular grandmothers—often, unfortunately, without sensitivity to those who find pain in this day
because they have wished to be mothers and are not.

This is where the day becomes difficult for the preacher. If
the pastor ignores the day completely, many will be disappointed and offended. But if the sermon is too narrowly focused
on biological motherhood, others will be just as deeply hurt.
Because church attendance is high on Mother's Day, and
because sentiment provides susceptible soil, it is a great day for
preaching. But it's also a perilous day because not everyone has
good memories of mother, and because a great many women
come to this day with lingering sadness—some because they've
never had children, and some because they feel they've failed as
mothers. So the preacher picks his or her way through a
homiletical minefield.

But above all, the preacher needs to remember that a sermon
should rarely, if ever, be dedicated to a minority of the congregation. A Mother's Day sermon ought to speak to parents in
general and to mothers in particular; but it ought also to speak
to every person in the congregation in some fashion. The
African wisdom "It takes a village to raise a child" should inform
the style of every Mother's Day and Father's Day sermon.

This sermon was preached at the Church of the Saviour
(United Methodist) in Cleveland, Ohio, in 1985—the thir-
teenth time I had ministered to that congregation on a Mother's
Day. I'd like to think that during those years I preached some
better ones, and I'm sure I preached some worse. But this sermon is quite typical of the approach I tried to follow—that is,
to honor the day but to get beyond it.

* * * *

OUR HOPE IS IN THE PAST GENERATION

Scripture Lesson: 2 Timothy 1:1–7

Every sports fan has encountered the "next season" philosophy. It works from whiffle ball to the big leagues, from sandlot football to the NFL. Big-league baseball fans discuss the young players on their farm clubs, building hope for next year. In professional football or basketball, they say, "Let's hope for a good draft next year." At the high school level, they sometimes reach out wildly: "Maybe some good athlete will move into our district." It's a simple, hopeful philosophy: "Things will be better next year." And there's a rule of thumb: the worse things are, the earlier in the season folks begin dreaming about next year.

But the sports world didn't invent this philosophy. We hear it every day. We're now at a place in the calendar when this theme reaches its peak. I'm speaking of commencement time, when all over the country, from middle school to university, speakers will tell us, "These young people (or these children) who stand before us today are the hope of the world."

I don't want to be a spoilsport, but I have to challenge that easy philosophy. I call it "easy" because it is an unconscious abdication of responsibility. The next generation is not our hope; our hope is in the *past* generation. Not the generation that's dead; no use looking there. I mean the generation that is seeking to abdicate—your generation, and mine. Nothing magic is going to happen to this next generation. It isn't like professional sports, where they hope to find a free agent or trade for a better place in the draft. Our human race has nowhere else to go. If there's to be a change, a winning season, we'll have to do the turning around. The next generation—our children—will do pretty much what we have trained and conditioned them to do. Don't hope for any magic.

In the late nineteenth century there was a great preacher in the South named Sam Jones. His style was as common as his name, and people usually got his point. One Sunday he preached on the subject "Home Religion." Four weeks later a man in his congregation sought him out. The man said he had gone home after that sermon and had studied his children, and after four weeks had reached a conclusion. "I found out," the farmer-businessman said, "that my children haven't got a single fault that I or their mother hasn't got, or a single virtue that we have not got; a direct copy of my wife and myself our children are."[1]

Well, our new understanding of the genetic code might alter slightly that farmer's conclusions, because we now know that a great many elements go into our children's makeup besides the direct contributions from mother and father. But the farmer was building his case not simply on heredity but even more on the teachings, example, and disciplines of his wife and himself. And he was right.

So if the future lies so much in the past—or, more specifically, in the present that is so rapidly slipping from us—and if the hope of tomorrow rests so heavily on the adults of today, what can be done? Plato, one of the classical philosophers, said that in the ideal state parenthood should be a privilege permitted only to those qualified in every way, but especially in their nobility of soul and character. One can't really argue with the sheer logic of Plato's case, but it's even easier to see its follies and perils. What committee or organization would decide which persons were so qualified? Who would determine the qualifications? Indeed, who would select the committee that would draw up the qualifications? But still more unnerving, isn't it fascinating to see how often God and nature seem to play tricks on our best planning? Perhaps you've heard of the letter the dancer Isadora Duncan is said to have written to George Bernard Shaw, suggesting that they join in having a child. She predicted 'a wonder,' with her body and Shaw's brains. Shaw replied, "Yes, but what if it had my body and your brains?"[2]

The truth is, God and nature have trusted the future indiscriminately to the human race. This trust is not restricted to the wise and the qualified, the people of character and ambition; almost anyone, qualified or not, can have children. A person of tragically low intelligence or of abominable character can engage in the mating process. Then, complicating the matter still more, we fallible humans are left with the responsibility of bringing up the babies who are born to us. When we're in our teens or early twenties, many of us are critical of our parents and the mistakes they made in raising us. When we get a little farther along in experience and are humbled and chastened by life, we decide our parents were not as inadequate as we thought. In fact, we begin to marvel that they did as well as they did, with what they had to work with.

So several facts emerge. For one, nature trusts the birthing and parenting experience to all kinds of humans, without regard for what we may consider to be their qualifications. Second, being a parent is hard work. It calls for an ingenious mix of intelligence, common sense, sensitivity, and endurance—to say nothing of a year-after-year financial investment! And third, the future of the human race lies in these adults who shape the lives of the young. It doesn't lie in the young, because they will be pretty much what we adults bend them to be. It is the adults who set the course.

But still I have to come back to a painful fact. Not all of these adults are going to do their job well. Some of them will be an utter disaster. Nor are the failures limited to any single class or level of education. And if there are so many who will do the job poorly, what can we do about it?

To begin with, those of us who are parents have to work all the more earnestly at our job, in the hope that we can take up some of the slack for those who fail. The late Dr. Robert McCracken said, "Parenthood is a *ministry* to which men and women are called by God."[3] Do you ever think of it that way? Do we realize that parenthood is a *calling from God*, for those who will so perceive it? I once knew a man, a Lutheran by faith, who taught in a middle school and operated a small summer business. One of his sons once asked him, "Dad, what is your goal in life?" My friend answered, "To put the hands of my family into the hand of God."

I can't imagine a higher calling or a more ultimate assignment. Our investment counselor may say, "Provide for your family's financial security." Yes, do, of course; but what shall it profit a child if he or she has a substantial inheritance but a fumbling, shriveled soul? The educator will advise us to give our children the finest possible education. I agree; few things mean more to me than my education. But if I speak and read in a dozen tongues and have sophisticated taste in music and art but am without character, I will be a plague on our human race. I know of nothing that is remotely as important as putting the hands of the next generation into the hands of God.

Our Scripture reading of the day is relatively brief, and the portion I want to discuss is still briefer. But short as the sentence is, its message to us is demanding. The apostle is writing to a young man in whom he sees great promise. I don't think it's inappropriate to say that Paul envisions this young man as his spiritual protégé; he was counting on him to carry on the work to which the apostle himself was so passionately dedicated. This letter to Timothy records the deepest convictions of a man who feels that his own life and ministry may well be near an end. But everything in the letter, it seems to me, rests on this sentence: "I am reminded of your sincere faith," the apostle writes to Timothy, "a faith that lived first in your grandmother Lois and your mother Eunice and now, I am sure, lives in you" (2 Timothy 1:5).

The apostle's expectations for Timothy are based not simply on his youthful energy or on his God-given gifts but on his family heritage of faith. It is a faith that has been passed on from grandmother to mother to Timothy. Here is the hope—that Timothy will carry on what past generations have given him. And here's an interesting detail. Timothy's father was a Greek, and apparently not a believer (Acts 16:1). We may rightly reason that Timothy's spiritual influences, therefore, depended largely on his mother and grandmother. At best, we want a child to be blessed with two parents who nurture his or her faith, but this isn't always the case. And thank God, stories like Timothy's number in the tens of thousands—instances where one parent or a parent and grandparent have laid the faith foundation.

In any event, the point is clear. Timothy is ready for his work with Paul because of the past generation; in fact, the past *two* generations. The apostle has hope for the next generation, but the hope exists because of the past generations.

So many parents take a detached attitude toward their children's faith journey. I'm speaking specifically of parents who are also church members; I wouldn't expect nonbelievers to recommend what they do not themselves claim. But I'm troubled when people who are presumably Christian say that they will leave their children's faith to their own decision. Ultimately, of course, the choice *is* personal; no one can accept Christ for another. But the parent, above all others, is the one to put the hand of a son or daughter into the hand of God.

But what about those who have no children, or those whose children are already grown and gone from home? Can we retire from the future of the human race if we fit into one of those categories? Not by any means! In a culture where children spend so much time outside the home, the influence of other adults is increasingly significant. I speak not only of aunts and uncles and grandparents, or of schoolteachers. Consider also the baby-sitter, the nursery school leader, neighbors, and youth workers—and also those people who give music, dance, and drama lessons.

Every child needs adult role models in addition to their own parents. There's a period in the lives of most young people when they're skeptical or even discrediting of the way their parents look at things. At such times it's important that teenagers have some worthy adults in their lives, persons whose character and conduct will influence them toward right values.

I was blessed with good parents, a gift for which I am eternally grateful. I can't remember ever really rebelling against them. As a matter of fact, I don't think I had that option! But I do remember with special gratitude the adults who rounded out my image of adult life. My parents were older than average; I'm thankful for a number of young adults, in their late twenties or thirties, who gave me a broader picture of what adults might be like. My parents were people of modest education; I'm thankful for teachers and ministers who gave me an image of formally educated adults. I'm sure there were a number of less tangible areas where my parents were limited, and though I never consciously sought adults who would fill those gaps, I'm nevertheless sure that some fine adults did so. When I ponder the mass of benefits that have blessed my life during my growing-up years, I have an almost endless list of adults.

Many were schoolteachers, whose role by definition is that of secondary parents, whether they wish it to be so or not. But beyond those teachers, the largest influence came from my church. And it was not only Sunday school teachers, though they stand high, but all those persons who stopped to talk with me after church, who noticed if I did something worthwhile in school, or who congratulated me when our boys' quartet sang; and the adults who came to our home for coffee and cake after church, and who encouraged me to be part of the conversation. My parents were my first line of faith and character, but they were supported by persons more numerous than I can ever record.

You and I can do that. We can help to pass some good thing to a generation that is soon coming into its own.

We live in a very difficult world. I grew up during the Great Depression, when Hitler and Mussolini were terrifying Europe; yet those days seem almost stable compared to our own, because personal morals and conduct were generally more predictable then, and while immorality existed, the media didn't flaunt it or give it credibility by their sometimes fawning attention. Homes, in those days, had more time to be homelike. Ours are not easy days to save a human soul or to make a mark for hope and peace.

But the prospects are good, if you and I will make them so. By "you and I," I mean especially those of us who are adults. But I also mean you young people who are here today, and who feel an impulse for right living. And we must begin now. We dare not wait for the next generation. Our hope lies with this generation here gathered.

So I want our church to do everything possible to make better *adults*. I'd like to have a dozen more Bible study groups, or prayer groups, or adult Sunday school classes. I'd like for us to do more programming in parenting, especially for us fathers. I'd like to have more settings in which faith can grow, and compassion, and self-understanding. And I want more and more opportunities of this kind for our junior and senior high kids, so they can get such a foundation under their lives that they will marry rightly and build their homes on a rock of faith.

If you want, you can abdicate from the human race just now by saying, "The next generation is the hope of the world." That's a belief in magic, like saying, "Abracadabra." For nothing really good is likely to happen in the next generation unless there is a birth of vital faith and commitment in this one.

Fortunately, there's still time for such a birth. We still have time to hug a child, to help a teenager get a scholarship, to take time to talk with a boy or a girl. Most of all, there's still time to live an exemplary life that will inspire observant children and young people to aim high. It's exciting to think that you and I can make such a difference.

Exciting, especially, to think that you and I might put the hand of some child or some young person into the hand of God.

NOTES

1. Sam P. Jones, "Quit Your Meanness," in *Twenty Centuries of Great Preaching*, ed. Clyde E. Fant Jr. and William M. Pinson Jr. (Waco, Tex.: Word Books, 1971), 6:338.
2. Clifton Fadiman and Andre Bernard, eds., *Bartlett's Book of Anecdotes* (Boston: Little, Brown and Co., 1985, 2000), 489.
3. Robert McCracken, "The Church in the Home," in *Twenty Centuries of Great Preaching*, 12:82–83.

10

Father's Day

Father's Day doesn't bless church attendance in the way Mother's Day does. We fathers would like to think this is because Father's Day comes during the summer, when church attendance tends to drop off, but this may be a fond hope.

Father's Day has come to have its own honored place in the popular calendar, but its path hasn't been as direct as that of its counterpart. Mrs. John Bruce Dodd started Father's Day in June 1910, and in 1936 a national Father's Day Committee was formed, but it was not until 1966 that a president, Lyndon B. Johnson, proclaimed the day. By that time, however, it was widely celebrated and had long had its recognized place in the calendar.

In my pastoral days, I didn't celebrate this holiday as faithfully as I did Mother's Day, and occasionally an earnest father told me so. But if it's difficult to walk the tightrope demanded of Mother's Day, the perils are even greater on Father's Day. One faces the parallel issue of those who wish they were fathers and are not. But one also faces the fact that fathers more often have an ambivalent place in memory, and that their role—like that of mothers—is in a state of flux in our culture.

I nearly always preached a series during summer months. This sometimes provided an opportunity to fold the father theme into a companion theme in the series, adding dimension and depth to both.

But by all means, respond at least some of the time to the Father's Day emphasis. Fathers need preaching to. Several significant studies indicate that boys, in particular, are not likely to find their place in the church except as their fathers do. The biblical pattern that expected the father to be a kind of priest-in-residence has much to commend it; and by extension, the role a man can play in the lives of children not his own is a highly important one. Most men are remarkably open to this message, when it is offered earnestly and positively.

This sermon was preached at a unique camp meeting in West Tennessee. When Howell Taylor moved to that area in the late 1820s, he immediately established a camp meeting that has been carried on every summer since. While anyone is welcome to attend the camp meeting, and many do, only descendants of the Taylor family can own "camps" on the grounds. As a result, the camp meeting is also a huge family reunion, and on the Sunday morning of the series, the camp president (always an ordained clergyperson from the family) baptizes a number of children. As someone who has been the guest preacher at rather frequent intervals since 1964, I knew the family quality of this day, and on a Sunday in 1998, I preached what was essentially a Father's Day sermon without the specific Father's Day references.

* * * *

THE THINGS WE DO FOR OUR CHILDREN

Scripture Lesson: Genesis 4:1–17

During the years that I was a pastor, I learned that a man is never more ready for serious thinking than at the birth of a first child. I speak of "serious thinking," but I should note that often it is also irrational thinking; serious, but careless of logical boundaries.

This is true no matter what kind of man he may be. A farmer of few words, a university professor, a business executive, a good old boy—he thinks deep thoughts at the birth of that first child. Sometimes he's surprised at himself. "I never thought it would mean this much to me. You know—I was serious about it. We talked about it a lot. And we wanted this baby. But I didn't know how it would hit me. Like a Mack truck."

Then, as I've already indicated, sometimes the new father does irrational things. If it's a boy, a father may go out and buy a football that's nearly as big as the baby. If it's a girl, the father sometimes confesses that he can already see her in her prom dress. Ogden Nash, whose poetry delighted so many during the middle of the twentieth century, contemplated the issue with mock seriousness when he looked at his baby daughter. Somewhere, he feared, there was a male infant peacefully at rest who will one day want to marry his daughter. For such a one, Nash promised,

> Sand for his spinach I'll gladly bring,
> And Tabasco sauce for his teething ring,[1]

Every father with an infant daughter knows the feeling.

The birth of a first child is harvesttime for insurance and investment advisers. They urge the new father to "do right by this little baby. Prepare for its future." And the father wants to—sometimes, wants to so much that he makes commitments beyond what he can really manage. He dreams of sending this child to college, contemplates piano lessons and insurance policies; even contemplates the eventual prospect of making a down payment on this infant's first car. The things we do for our children!

This feeling goes back a long, long way. I suspect it's as old as the human race. I have evidence it traces back all the way to the biblical character named Cain. Let me tell you the story.

I should mention at the outset that Cain wasn't an admirable character. He was ignoble in the way he felt about his brother, Abel; in the way he responded to God's warning; in the killing of his brother; and in the way he responded to God's inquiry after the murder. The only redeeming feature I find in Cain is in the way he felt when his first child was born.

But before I can tell you about that, I need to summarize the earlier parts of the story. Cain was the first son of Adam and Eve. His birth was a very big deal, though in his case we know more about his mother's feelings than about his father's. Eve said, when Cain was born, "I have produced a man with the help of the Lord" (Genesis 4:1). Bible scholars generally feel that this was Eve's way of saying that she thought she had brought into the world the one that would bring revenge on the serpent that had led her and Adam astray. Unfortunately, it was not to be so. Indeed, it turned out quite the opposite. Cain seemed more like the serpent than like one who would defeat the serpent.

We know nothing about Cain's growing up, except we have reason to think he slowly developed feelings of jealousy for his younger brother, Abel. And why not? Older siblings have monopoly on their parents' affection until a small intruder lays claim to not only a part of their attention but a large and insistent part. We can only speculate on this, but I'm very sure that when Cain and Abel came as adults to the event reported in the book of Genesis, Cain already had a good bit of emotional baggage. The kind of feelings Cain eventually showed toward Abel aren't born in a moment; they have a long ancestry, and usually a complicated one.

As they became adults, Cain became a tiller of the soil and Abel a keeper of sheep. We can assume they were both rather successful; after all, the soil was virgin and the flocks hadn't yet developed hereditary diseases. Both men were at least nominally religious. We don't know what their parents taught them or how clearly God had been revealed to them. But they were religious enough that they came to give an offering to God. And they gave, of course, the only thing they had. Their only currency was farm produce, and they gave it.

Again, we don't know many details, but we do know the heart of the matter. We read that "the Lord had regard for Abel and his offering, but for Cain and his offering [God] had no regard" (Genesis 4:4–5). A New Testament writer tells us the difference: Abel made a better sacrifice than his brother because his was marked by faith (Hebrews 11:4). We don't know why Cain had a poorer grade of faith. Perhaps it was because he was fuming over old resentments and jealousies. I repeat, our sins usually have some ancestry.

Nor do we know how it is that Cain sensed that Abel was accepted while he was not. Perhaps it was a look of rapturous blessing on Abel's face. If your soul is in a bad mood, few things are more irritating than to see someone with eyes closed, face lit, adoring God, while you feel nothing. And the feeling is all the more intense when the happy someone is someone for whom you already have some inclination toward resentment. Maybe that's what happened to Cain.

Anyway, Cain became angry, and "his countenance fell" (Genesis 4:5). At this moment, God was very good to Cain. God might justifiably have said, "Stop your petulance!" Instead, God asked kindly, "Why are you angry, and why has your countenance fallen? If you do well, will you not be accepted? And if you do not do well, sin is lurking at the door; its desire is for you, but you must master it" (Genesis 4:6–7). Here was grace. God was convicting Cain, telling him kindly that if he got his soul in order, he could be just as happy as his brother Abel—and God warned him that if he did not, he would be the victim of sin.

(One wonders if Cain's parents ever told him stories of their initial experience with sin. Of did they perhaps never share their painful story? I wonder if Cain knew how dangerous sin is. And did he know that sin gets its start in the mind, but that it rarely stops there?)

You remember what happened next. Cain, ignoring God's counsel, asked his brother to go with him into the field, and there, out of sight of everyone but God, Cain killed his brother. It was murder—not self-defense, not manslaughter, but murder. Premeditated, cold-blooded murder.

When God confronted him in his crime, Cain tried to slip out of the matter, but his effort was pathetic and amateurish. God told him that from this time forward the ground would never again "yield to you its strength," and also that he would be "a fugitive and a wanderer" (Genesis 4:12). Cain now feared that someone would take his life, just as he had taken Abel's. This is one of the subtle by-products of sin: we come to fear that others will do to us what we have done to someone else. We begin (not surprisingly) to judge others by the quality of our own character. When you stop to think of it, that's a very fearful penalty all by itself. It's not the worst of the results of our sinning, but it's a very sorry one.

But the Lord put a mark on Cain, so no one would kill him. We don't know what the mark was. It would save his life, but it was hardly a red badge of courage. I'm sure it was a mark that would embarrass Cain, even while it protected him.

So Cain went far away, to the land of Nod, east of Eden. There he tried to start a new life. He and his wife conceived, and they had a son. And the Bible says, "And he built a city, and named it Enoch, after his son" (Genesis 4:17).

I submit that this is the first recorded instance of a person doing something special for a newborn child. Not a season ticket to be used ten years later at a Green Bay Packers game, not a college annuity program, not an item to be read after his death, but a city! He built a city, and named it for his son! No twenty-first-century entrepreneur could celebrate the event with a greater flourish.

The Bible, in its often laconic fashion, doesn't tell us anything about the city. It reveals nothing about its size or its quality. We don't know if it was a village or a full-blown city, if it was situated on a river, or if it had suburbs. But it *does* tell us that Cain built a city, and why he built it; he named it for his son. And that's important. Because the Bible doesn't say things casually. If the Bible includes details, you can figure that they matter. The details tell us we should pay attention. And the writer of Genesis tells us that Cain built a city, and named it for his son. The things we do for our children!

Why do you think Cain built a city for his son? We could write it off as sheer opulence, an act of supreme braggadocio. But I don't think so. Even when we brag, we choose bragging that fits—perhaps especially about something we think is missing from life, especially our life. I had a friend, a delightful man, who became a successful salesman. He told me how he grew up in a very poor neighborhood in Chicago, and how he used to watch the big cars that sometimes motored through. He resolved, as a boy, that someday he would drive just such a car. So one day he bought a very large, very white Cadillac and drove to Chicago, wending slowly down the street where he had been poor. Yes, even when we're going to boast, we choose our venue.

So what did Cain have in mind? Did he never get over feeling like an outcast? And did he want to make sure that his son wouldn't ever have to feel that way? How better to do so than to build a city and give it his son's name? You can't be an outcast when it's your town, when your name is over the gate and on the border signs! What a gift to give your son, to deliver him from your shame—the shame he might well inherit.

I wonder, too, if the gift had anything to do with the mark that was on Cain. As I said earlier, we don't know what that mark was, but we can well realize that even though it protected him, it also *marked* him. Perhaps this city was to compensate for that mark. And it's interesting that Cain didn't name the city for himself; he named it for his son. I think he wanted his son to be free of the burden of his father, and of his father's name.

And I can't help wondering if Cain, in building a city and naming it for his son, was still at odds with God. Was his building a city and naming it for his son an act of arrogance, even if exercised through his son? Cain, after all, was condemned to be a fugitive and a wanderer all his life. In building a city for his son, was Cain trying to do an end run on God? He knew better than to assert himself by naming the city for himself. But was he trying to slip by in using his son's name? And this stuff about a city—cities don't have a good reputation in the early chapters of Genesis. Was Cain making a statement by building a city?

Ah, the things we do for our children! Especially this: we so often do through them what we weren't able to do for ourselves. How many a born violinist has been forced to go out for the football team his father never made? How many a girl has worn the wedding dress and had the folderol that her mother wasn't able to have for her own wedding? How often our children become extensions of our frustrations.

So Cain built a city and named it for his son. Quite a birthday gift, you have to admit.

But not the one I wish Cain had made. I wish he had built an altar for his son. Because, you see, this is where Cain's life really, tragically went wrong. I wish he had built an altar. And I wish that even before his son was fully weaned, Cain had begun taking him there. And I wish that one day, as soon as the boy was old enough to understand, Cain had said to him, "Son, this is an altar. It is the most important object in all of creation. I misused it when I was young, and my mistake has ruined my life. See this mark on me, Son? I wouldn't have it, if I had known enough to make right use of an altar. Your uncle Abel, whom you never knew—he'd be here playing ball with you and me now, if I had done the right kind of business at the altar.

"So I want you to have an altar. It's the biggest thing I can give you. An altar."

I wish Cain had said that to his son, Enoch. And I wish you and I would say something like that to our sons and daughters. The things we do for our children! And only one thing is utterly essential: to give them an altar, where they will come to know the living God.

NOTES

1. Ogden Nash, *Selected Poetry of Ogden Nash* (New York: Black Dog & Leventhal, 1995), 91–92.

11

Trinity Sunday

Throughout my rather long pastoral ministry, I prided myself on offering my people a balanced pulpit diet. I tried carefully to honor both the personal and social elements of the gospel, to make my preaching both pastoral and prophetic, and to range widely over the whole body of Scripture.

So I was humbled by a June Sunday in London, England, in 1999. In the morning, my wife, Janet, and I worshiped in an Anglican church in the neighborhood of our hotel, and in the evening at Central Hall, the Methodist meeting place in Westminster. In each church, the sermon celebrated Trinity Sunday. During the morning service, I acknowledged to myself that I had not, in all my years of preaching, celebrated Trinity Sunday, and in the evening service I repented thereof with great embarrassment. I realized I had not been as faithful a pastor-preacher as I had thought myself to be. I wish I could suggest that like the eleventh-century pope, Alexander II, I felt Trinity Sunday should not be observed because the Trinity is honored on every day of the church year; but it would not be true. Like most pastors, I simply found the Trinity a difficult subject on which to preach, and consciously or unconsciously, I walked around it.

Trinity Sunday is unique in the church calendar in that it is the only special day in the church year that celebrates a doc trine rather than an event. That fact, of itself, indicates the importance of the doctrine and, in turn, shames us for neglecting the doctrine in our preaching.

From sometime in the tenth century, this Sunday was celebrated in many places on the Sunday after Pentecost, but it was not until 1334 that it was generally observed in the Western church. In the Eastern Orthodox church, the Trinity is honored at Pentecost.

No doubt, one of the particular benefits of attending to the calendar is that the preacher is reminded of subjects he or she might otherwise neglect. Also, the preacher finds justification for approaching subjects that parishioners may see as peripheral. When the sermon can begin, "Today is Trinity Sunday," the topic is not odd but authorized.

Several familiar hymns celebrate the members of the Trinity in successive verses. I worshiped recently in a church where the congregation first sang a hymn celebrating the Trinity, then, consecutively, a verse each from three hymns honoring Father, Son, and Holy Spirit, respectively. The effect was particularly strengthening, it seemed to me.

There are many exotic and exciting ways to approach the subject of the Trinity. I have chosen in this sermon to be rather basic, which is a posture I would recommend for a good deal of Trinity preaching.

I have not preached this sermon—not yet, at least. I have prepared it for this book as a penance for so many neglected Trinity Sundays.

* * * *

NAMING A MYSTERY

Scripture Lesson: John 14:15–21, 25–28

Today is Trinity Sunday, one of the major days of the church calendar. Most of our church days commemorate some event—Christmas, Easter, and Pentecost. But Trinity Sunday celebrates a *doctrine*. If one is just a wee bit logical, one says, "The doctrine must be quite important if there's a special day to celebrate it," and I have to answer, "You're right. This is, indeed, an important doctrine." As doctrines go, the Trinity is probably our most distinctive Christian doctrine. I didn't say it's the most important; that would be a stretch. But it is our most distinctive, that is, the doctrine that most clearly defines us from other religious bodies.

I think of it this way. We're often reminded these days that Judaism, Christianity, and Islam are the world's three great monotheistic religions—that is, religions that believe in one God. But Christianity is crucially different from Judaism and Islam in that while we, too, believe in one God, we believe that God is expressed in the Trinity. This is so central to who we are that when the first great Reformation movement, the followers of Martin Luther, presented a confession of faith to the Diet of the Holy Roman Empire in 1530, the first article was the doctrine of the Trinity. And something like a century later, when the Church of England separated from the Roman Catholic Church and drew up its formal statement of beliefs, the first doctrine in the statement was the Holy Trinity. This is who we are; we're a *Trinitarian* people.

So it's appropriate on this Trinity Sunday that I should talk with you about the doctrine of the Trinity. And if I know anything about you, I'm quite sure some of you are saying just now, "Is that really necessary? It's so hard to understand that I think you'll just leave me confused."

Well, if you think this is hard for you to understand, imagine how the first disciples felt. And here's the interesting part: Jesus never attempted to explain the Trinity to his disciples; he just referred to it matter-of-factly, as if they already knew all about it. I'm thinking of our Scripture lesson of the day. Jesus said to the disciples, "I will ask the Father, and he will give you another Advocate, to be with you forever." I think the disciples had a partial basis for understanding this statement. They surely must have sensed for some time that Jesus was their advocate—that is, that he was always pleading their case and their cause. And not theirs only, but the case and cause of all the diseased, the downtrodden, the demon-distressed. Now he was saying that he would be sending them *another* Advocate, and that this Advocate would be with them *forever*. An interesting idea; but who would this be? So Jesus went on, without a pause, to say that this Advocate "is the Spirit of truth," someone the world can't receive because it "neither sees him nor knows him." Then Jesus made it still more mysterious and complicated. But "[y]ou know him," Jesus explained, "because he abides with you, and he will be in you" (John 14:16–18).

Well, as I said a moment ago, if you think the Trinity is confusing to you, think how it must have struck those first disciples. They were all Jews, which means that they had deep convictions about the nature and character of God, and about the fact that God is *one*. Now their great teacher was telling them that the Spirit was going to be *in* them—which strongly suggested that God was going to be in them. This was not only hard for them to understand; I think it was something they weren't even sure that they wanted to understand. This had to seem like dangerous knowledge.

And Jesus wasn't done. He went on to say that he would soon be gone, but that they would still see him. And more than that: "On that day you will know that I am in my Father, and you in me, and I in you" (John 14:20). And still more: "I have said these things to you while I am still with you. But the Advocate, the Holy Spirit, whom the Father will send in my name, will teach you everything, and remind you of all that I have said to you" (John 14:25–26). Did you get that? I wonder if the disciples did. In one breath, Jesus spoke of the Holy Spirit, the Father, and himself and said that God would send the Holy Spirit in his— that is, Jesus'—name. This was pretty heady stuff for these

Jews, who believed deeply that God is one, because Jesus was putting God, himself, and the Holy Spirit into one package, as if they were all in business together.

Some weeks later, after the crucifixion and the resurrection, when Jesus was giving some final instructions to his disciples, he used the same kind of language: "Go therefore," he told his disciples, "and make disciples of all nations, baptizing them in the name of the Father and of the Son and of the Holy Spirit" (Matthew 28:19).

See how naturally Jesus talked about the Trinity. He didn't use the term, but he referred to the three persons in the God-head as if his disciples understood what he was talking about. He dared to speak about something so perplexing as his being one with the Father, and about the coming of the Holy Spirit. And it looks as if the disciples got it, because less than two weeks later, on the day of Pentecost, Simon Peter picked up the whole wonderful theme as he spoke to the huge crowd that had gathered to see what was going on. He told them that Jesus was now "exalted at the right hand of God," and that he had "received from the Father the promise of the Holy Spirit," which he had now poured out upon this group of his followers. And when the people, deeply convicted, asked what they should do, Peter again mixed together these three personalities. Repent, Peter said, in the name of *Jesus Christ*, and you will receive the *Holy Spirit*, whom the *Lord our God* has promised to all that call upon him (Acts 2:33, 38).

So the disciples have gotten hold of something that is undeniably real and, in its own way, profoundly logical. They know that God is one, but that God is also Father, Son, and Holy Spirit. And they know this not simply as a theological formula but as a fact of their experience. As faithful Jews, they had always believed in God. Slowly, they had come to realize that Jesus the Christ was also God. Indeed, whatever they now knew about God, of this they were utterly sure: having seen Jesus, they had seen God. Jesus himself had dared to tell them so, when Philip asked to see the Father. "Whoever has seen me has seen the Father," Jesus answered (John 14:9). Still more, they had now been filled with the Holy Spirit; God had now dwelled in them. God was one and indivisible, no doubt about that. But God was also their Lord Christ and the Holy Spirit.

This is a mystery, no doubt about it. What do you call it? What shall you name this mystery? The early church, in time, named this mystery the Trinity. As far as we know, a late second-century theologian, Theophilus of Antioch, was the first person to use a word like *trinity* to describe this doctrine, but the idea had been there from the beginning. And what better name could there be? *Trinity: tri-unius*; three, yet one; three in one; one in three. This is our Christian name for the mystery of God, as God is revealed to us in the Scriptures and in our human experience.

When you think about it, you realize that it isn't out of the ordinary for us to get hold of a reality before we have a name for it. This a pretty universal experience. Humans knew there was something like *love* before even the most ancient peoples had a word for it. We understood the wonder of sunrise and sunset, trees, lakes, and mountains, long before our ancestors gave us the word *beautiful*. Humans perceived a magnificent element of character long before they got a word like *honor* to encapsulate it. We're always looking for words big enough to carry the freight of some things we know to be true. It's our good fortune, in the Christian faith, that we were blessed with theologians to give us such a name as Trinity to describe God.

And yet—I don't know why I should conclude that it was a theologian who first gave us the word *trinity*. Mind you, theologians preserved the word by putting it into writing; but who can say who first enunciated the term? Maybe it was a passing troubadour who was trying to sing the faith he or she had experienced. Or perhaps a devout shopkeeper found the figure of speech when discussing theology with a friend; or a mother, perhaps, trying to initiate her child into the wonders of God that she had come to know. After all, we're told that Saint Patrick explained the Trinity to the Irish by way of the three-leaf clover; who knows how simply some unknown person first cast the idea in the word, before a theologian enunciated it?

But the more the first Christians lived with the idea, the more they knew that it had always been. They remembered the story of the creation, and how it was that God, in the beginning, created the heavens and the earth; but that it was the Spirit of God that breathed on the waters. And when the New Testament writer, in John's Gospel, explained the event, he said that the Word was there when the creation took place, and that the Word was the one who eventually became flesh and dwelt among us as the Christ. The early Christians came to realize that there was always a Trinity but that the picture was not clear until Jesus Christ, and until the unique visitation of the Holy Spirit on the Day of Pentecost. And when the church found itself with too big a mystery for any word previously in their vocabulary, they found a word: *trinity*. They named the mystery Trinity.

But you're a practical soul, full of pragmatic considerations. You want to ask me what difference all this makes. What does the doctrine of the Trinity matter to a guy or a gal who has to go to work or to school tomorrow, the day after Trinity Sunday? So what? you wish you could say to me.

And I will answer: So a lot! A lot more than I can tell you on one Sunday. In truth, a lot more than I *know*, so I'm very sure I can't tell it to you in one Sunday, or in all the Sundays that might come my way. But let me take you back to the text of the day, to tell you just one small but very important part of what this all means to you and to me. I'm thinking of a wonderful little sentence. Jesus said to his disciples, "I will not leave you orphaned" (John 14:18). As Jesus talked with his disciples about everything that was soon to happen, he wanted to reassure them about one fact: he would still be with them.

From our very human point of view, this is the essence of the doctrine of the Trinity: God desires to be with us. God desires so much for this to be the case as to constantly reach out to us. God creates our universe so that, if we are willing, we can see God all about us in the wonders of creation. But this is both mechanical and overwhelming, so God comes to us in the flesh, in the presence of the Son. But this incarnational visit is limited by time and space, so God comes among us by means of the

Holy Spirit. Indeed, more than that, God offers to dwell in us by the Spirit.

The doctrine of the Trinity teaches many things about both the nature and the person of God; more than I can say today. But find gladness in this: that each time you say, "God in three persons, blessed Trinity," you are declaring God's holy desire to be related to the universe in general, and particularly to us human creatures.

The doctrine of the Trinity is a mystery, no question about it. But it is a lovely mystery, because one of the things it tells us about God is that God loves, God cares, and God seeks from eternity to eternity to relate to our human race. God never will leave us orphaned. The Trinity says so.

12

Pentecost

Early in the twentieth century, a fine British preacher and educator, Samuel Chadwick, said that no doctrine of the Christian faith is as neglected as the doctrine of the Holy Spirit. Contemporary observers might argue that this is no longer the case, because of the growth of the Pentecostal and charismatic movements. While those movements have given great prominence to certain expressions of the work of the Holy Spirit, I'm not sure that the basic doctrine itself is any better emphasized or understood. Pentecost Sunday should encourage the preacher to lead the people of God in considering the wondrous message of the Holy Spirit.

But since Pentecost is also the birthday of the church, this Sunday is a grand opportunity for some solid ecclesiology. Here is another doctrine easily neglected, particularly in our time, when individualism has become a powerful but unwritten doctrine for so many in the church; in fact, individualism may well be one of the most popular heresies of our time. A thoughtful homiletician will do well on occasion to combine the two themes—the Holy Spirit and the church. After all, they belong together. But for sure, the preacher should find in Pentecost Sunday an opportunity to rejoice in the fact of the church. What better time than the birthday of the church to give thanks for its potential and essential glory? No one denies that the church, as experienced, is not all it ought to be; it is important, therefore, to remind ourselves of all that God has intended us to be.

The Pentecost festival has its roots in the Old Testament, in the Feast of Firstfruits and the Feast of Weeks (Exodus 23:16; Leviticus 23:15–21). For Christians, the word recalls the outpouring of the Holy Spirit, and with it the empowering of the church to declare the message of the risen Christ. Christians have celebrated Pentecost Sunday since at least the third century. Tertullian encouraged baptism during the entire fifty days leading to Pentecost. As a result, in the English tradition, the day is often called Whitsunday (White Sunday), because those who were newly baptized wore their white robes on that day. The image of whiteness offers some picturesque insights for the homiletical mind.

All of this suggests that the preacher may have to choose among a number of important and exciting themes on this day. From a pragmatic point of view, it is unfortunate that Pentecost often has to compete with Mother's Day, Memorial Day, or Father's Day, as well as the sometimes-diminished attendance of early summer.

The sermon that follows is one I have not yet preached. I wish I had preached more often on the theme of the Holy Spirit. And though I included the church rather faithfully in my preaching regimen, I think I did not do as well as I should have with the basic doctrine of the church—which is to say, I wish I had done more with Pentecost.

* * * *

BEHIND THE SPIRITUAL TIMES

Scripture Lesson: Acts 19:1–7

If it weren't for the adjective in my sermon title, many of you would find my subject more interesting. No one wants to be "behind the times." We want to be with it! We want to be cutting-edge. We want to know tomorrow's headlines before they're printed. So yes, you'd hate to be behind the times. But "behind the *spiritual* times"? Who cares? For that matter, who even knows what that means?

It will take me a while to tell you something of what it means. But as for who cares, you and I should care, and should care desperately. You and I are not simply physical beings, and we're not simply intellectual beings; we are also spiritual creatures. And I dare to suggest that it's the spiritual part of us that is the most important, because the spiritual plays such a huge role in what happens to us physically and intellectually. Isn't it interesting that we pay so much attention to our physical welfare—what we wear, what we eat, what the doctor says about our bodies—and at least a little bit to our intellectual welfare—getting an education; reading books, newspapers, and periodicals; catching some worthwhile programs on radio or television—and yet we give so little concern to our spiritual welfare?

Well, it's not quite fair to make such an accusation to you, because you're in church, and your being in church indicates that you do, indeed, give some thought to spiritual matters; otherwise you wouldn't be here today. Nevertheless, my sermon title may well apply to you—and for that matter, it may apply to me more than I want to confess. It's quite possible that you and I are behind the spiritual times.

I take the phrase from Dr. John Henry Jowett, one of the great preachers in the first years of the twentieth century, famous both in the United States and in the British Isles. Jowett was talking about the incident referred to in our Scripture lesson of the day. Let me remind you of the story.

In the course of one of his missionary journeys, the apostle Paul came to the city of Ephesus. Paul was a pioneering preacher, so he tried to go to places where the gospel had not yet been heard. But to his delight, and perhaps to his surprise, Paul found some believers in Ephesus. I get the feeling, however, that very soon he sensed something missing in these disciples. The biblical writer doesn't say so, but it's certainly implied by Paul's question: "Did you receive the Holy Spirit when you became believers?" (Acts 19:2). And these believers—about twelve of them, the writer says—answered, "No, we have not even heard that there is a Holy Spirit."

That's the conversation that made Jowett say that these people were "behind the spiritual times." The Day of Pentecost had already come, but they didn't know there was such a fact as the Holy Spirit.[1]

Well, here it is Pentecost Sunday, and it seems appropriate to raise the same question for us, here. I wonder, if we took a poll, how many of us would have to say—for all practical purposes—that we hardly know there is a Holy Spirit. Mind you, we sing the Gloria Patri, which includes a reference to the Holy Spirit, and we mention the Holy Spirit each time we have a baptism, and quite often the Holy Spirit is named at some point during the benediction or some other blessing. But what does that mean to us? Do we hear the words as no more than a phrase from a mystical formula—in our own language, surely, but for all practical purposes like a foreign tongue? The people at Ephesus had an excuse. They literally hadn't heard of the Holy Spirit. We've heard the term, the name, but I fear that we live our Christian lives rather as if the Holy Spirit did not exist—or at least, didn't really matter.

Why was Paul so insistent that these disciples at Ephesus should receive the Holy Spirit? And why, indeed, would he have the same insistence for us? Wasn't it enough that these people were followers of Jesus Christ? Over the years I have always asked the students in my confirmation classes—seventh-graders—"What is a Christian?" And almost without fail, they've answered, "Someone who believes in God." I've always had to get them beyond that definition. One can believe in God and be a Jew or a Muslim or, for that matter, a person of no commitment whatsoever. Something more is involved in being a Christian, namely, that one accepts Jesus Christ as Savior and as Lord of life.

But if Saint Paul had been meeting with my young confirmands, he wouldn't have stopped there. He wouldn't have been satisfied with their knowing about Jesus Christ. He would have asked my confirmands the same question he asked the people at Ephesus: Have you received the Holy Spirit since you believed?

Come to think of it, neither would Paul be fully happy with the statistics we keep in our churches. We report annually how many members we have, how many attend worship and special classes, and how many have been baptized. But I doubt that there is any major church body that has a statistical line titled "How many have received the Holy Spirit?"

All of this would trouble the apostle Paul, and if it would trouble him, it should trouble us. Even if our pride hates to confess it, Paul pretty clearly knows more about the doctrinal issues of the church than we do, and he thought the role of the Holy Spirit in the Christian life was crucial. But why? I think we have a right to ask why. The Christian life is a life of obedience, but it isn't really blind obedience, so we want to know why the Holy Spirit is so important that the first question the premier apostle asked these earnest followers of Jesus is whether they had received the Holy Spirit.

Well, one thing is sure: Jesus made a big point of it, so when Paul raised the question, he was simply reflecting his Lord. When Jesus was about to depart this earth, he ordered his disciples not to leave Jerusalem but to wait there for "the promise of the Father," the baptism of the Holy Spirit. And when his disciples began raising questions about the future, Jesus essentially said, "That's none of your concern. 'But you will receive power when the Holy Spirit has come upon you; and you will be my witnesses in Jerusalem, in all Judea and Samaria, and to the ends of the earth'" (Acts 1:4–5, 6–8). From what Jesus said, we have to conclude that the whole assignment he was giving his followers depended on their having the Holy Spirit. They wouldn't be able to do what he expected them to do unless the Holy Spirit had come into their lives in a unique way.

That was the word for the first followers of Jesus. Now the question is, do we still need the Holy Spirit today? Some of you might answer, rather logically, that the first believers had a need that was greater than ours. Christianity was a new thing, and they were going to face persecution on all sides. And if you reason that way, you have a point. I suspect our fellow Christians in many parts of the world would be quick to tell us that you can't survive in the midst of fierce persecution unless your faith is firmly grounded—that is, unless the Holy Spirit is a very real fact in your life. I remember meeting a missionary many years ago who had just been released from a Chinese Communist prison, where he had spent several torturous years. He said that the only Christians who will survive such treatment are those for whom their faith is more than a philosophy; for whom it is a burning reality.

Does that mean, then, that American Christians can make it without the Holy Spirit? Perhaps that depends on what kind of Christian we want to be. In truth, I sense that the lines of conflict are being more sharply drawn every day. Because of the rise of the evangelical movement, Christianity in America is more vigorously visible than it has been in perhaps a century, and this, in turn, has caused more outspoken opposition. Common expressions of Christianity are frequently taken to court. In my high school days, a long generation ago, virtually all the music that was sung by our a cappella choir in our public high school was Christian music—great chorales in the Lutheran tradition or majestic music in Latin from the Catholic heritage. Such music is often discouraged today in public schools. This same principle of exclusion is at work today in a wide variety of ways in American public life, and it's clear that many powerful forces intend for a common Christian presence to be steadily diminished.

This means that the Christian witness is going to depend increasingly on the vitality and the deep-down reality of individual Christians. We will get less and less help from the culture itself. And in a way, this isn't all bad. Christianity needs to be seen for what it truly is: not simply as part of the American way of life or as part of our Western culture but as a transforming fact in individual human lives, and as a redeeming way of life—and eventually, in the whole quality of our culture, not because of our numbers or our political influence but because of the unique integrity and quality of our lives.

But this will happen only if we individual believers become more vitally Christian. I think of a phrase that Saint Paul used, "the fruit of the Spirit." He was speaking of such matters as love, joy, peace, patience, kindness, and gentleness. We use these words in our common vocabulary, but most of us will agree that we don't really see much demonstration of these virtues. And worse, I strongly suspect that we may not even have a clear definition of these virtues. That is, I wonder if we see enough *true* love, joy, peace, kindness, and gentleness to know what the authentic article is. Perhaps we have become programmed to plastic virtues, or to a kind of earnest imitation.

But even our quite secular culture recognizes that plastic virtues are not enough. One realizes as much when a Mother Teresa comes along. I am impressed that Catholic, Protestant, and pagan alike were in awe of the quality they saw in that little Albanian nun. And it seems to me that the way people responded to Mother Teresa indicates the very real hunger in our society for truly good human beings. We're quite tired of sham, of heroes produced by a public relations machine. We will accept them (as poor substitutes) if we're given nothing better, but we're hungry for reality, the sort of reality that comes in persons who are filled with the Holy Spirit.

We can't produce such reality without the help of the Holy Spirit. People might have made a valiant try in another time, but the secularity and the inherent crudeness of so much of our culture demand that we get reality.

And that's the secret genius of the Holy Spirit. The Holy Spirit is not something one puts on from the outside. Neither is it something one learns in some sort of finishing school—not even a religious finishing school! The Holy Spirit is something that happens to us *within*. This is the very language of the Bible with regard to the Holy Spirit. So we read that Jesus *breathed* on his disciples and said, "Receive the Holy Spirit," and that on the Day of Pentecost those present were all "filled with the Holy Spirit" (John 20:22; Acts 2:4). Here is the unique power and wonder of the Holy Spirit. The Spirit is not something we put on, or that we strive for, or that we imitate; it is God dwelling within us, uniquely and pervasively.

And that is what we need in our day and time. "The world is too much with us," the poet said in a simpler time, "late and soon, / Getting and spending." If that was true in Wordsworth's day, two centuries ago, heaven alone knows how true it is today—and how much, therefore, we need the power of the Holy Spirit in our daily lives.

There isn't time in this sermon to talk about how we receive the Holy Spirit. I'm very sure there is no formula, because God isn't manipulated or controlled by our systems. I want only to say this: God *wants* us to enjoy the power of the Holy Spirit in our lives; this is why God's Spirit is in the world. And I'm sure that any truly effective presence of the Holy Spirit is not simply a single experience, no matter how valid and wonderful that experience may be. The Holy Spirit is a continuing presence, and we are responsible to provide a setting where the Holy Spirit receives a continuing hospitality. That means a certain real and faithful earnestness on our part. For that reason, the message of the Spirit-filled life is a message for the long haul.

Most of us, I fear, are behind the times spiritually. Pentecost has come, and some of us, for all practical purposes, are no better off than those first-century believers in Ephesus; we've hardly realized that there *is* a Holy Spirit. Well, today—Pentecost Sunday—is a magnificent day to get on the right track. Today, please God, we will start getting up to date with God's purposes. We will become serious about the Holy Spirit.

NOTES

1. J. H. Jowett, *The Passion for Souls* (New York: Fleming H. Revell Co., 1905), 76.

13

Independence Day

Many preachers studiously avoid Independence Day because of their concern with the very real dangers of civil religion. But we shouldn't be so cautious about misuse or abuse that we miss the opportunity for proper celebration. The Scriptures are not embarrassed by the fact that we live in a civil society and that we participate in forms of government. The Old Testament is altogether comfortable in relating God with government. Obviously we have to translate its concepts from theocracy into our patterns of a democratic republic, but in doing so we can still lay claim to some powerful metaphors. The New Testament called the people of God to a right relationship with government, even when the government was other than they wanted it to be. Jesus' enemies hoped to embarrass him with the question "Shall we pay taxes to Caesar?" (see Luke 20:22). Jesus' succinct reply still challenges our basic citizenship twenty centuries later. Paul lived under a government that was often despotic and at times demonic, yet he called believers to "be subject to the governing authorities" (Romans 13:1). And as for his personal position, he confessed gladly that he was "a citizen of an important city" (Acts 21:39), and he didn't hesitate to claim the full rights of his Roman citizenship (Acts 16:37).

In total, the Scriptures won't allow us to be independent of government on the one hand or to be civil sycophants on the other. Because we recognize the fallen state of our human race, we know both our need of government and the fallibility of government, constituted as it is of humans. We are called therefore to a tenuous relationship. Christian citizenship is a moving target. The Christian pulpit must be sensitive to that fact and never abdicate its calling.

The Sunday nearest Independence Day provides a strategic opportunity for fulfilling this calling. Probably the preacher's basic posture is that of the loyal opposition. We ought to be the most exemplary of citizens. Someone has said that the best citizen is not the one who says, "My country, right or wrong," but the one who strives always to direct his or her country to the right.

To do so, preachers need to be reasonably good students of their nation's history. That's no simple task just now. We're in a period of vigorous historical revisionism, so the preacher will want to be intelligently sure of any historical references. This means that the preacher must avoid doctrinaire political positions. We are responsible, above all, to be captive to Christ, not to a particular political party or a particular philosophical position. It isn't easy to steer our homiletical ship through all the biblical, doctrinal, historical, and political data, and with it all to remain interesting, even to speak with prophetic clarity. But whoever said that preaching was supposed to be easy?

I think it is crucial that something about the sermon, whether in the language or content of the sermon itself or in the preacher's manner, should make clear that the preacher is not speaking from a superior, judgmental position. As with all sermons, the preacher should be speaking from within the addressed body, not as an outsider pointing a finger. Much of this has to do with manner of delivery, but the delivery is tilted by the words and concepts.

The sermon "Our Gold Refined" was preached at the venerable Chautauqua Institution in upstate New York. Chautauqua has a long history of political sophistication. President Ulysses S. Grant visited there in 1875, when the institution was only a year old, and for some two generations after that, nearly every president visited there at least once, either as candidate or incumbent. Probably the most memorable such visit was the occasion of Franklin Roosevelt's "I Hate War" speech in

August, 1936. In any event, the audiences at Chautauqua are accustomed to hearing national affairs discussed by a variety of economists, political scientists, media pundits, and public personalities. In this respect they are a receptive audience, but also a quite knowledgeable one. I couldn't hope to speak with the authority of their usual platform personalities. But I didn't expect to. I saw myself as a minister of the gospel, seeking to look at our nation, on the occasion of Independence Day, from the vantage point of the Christian faith.

This is our unique platform. It is presumptuous to compare ourselves with the Old Testament prophets, but we work in that tradition. Implicitly or explicitly, we ought to contribute to the conscience of our community, and to its political and economic structures. A day such as Independence Day provides an ideal setting for such an expression.

* * * *

OUR GOLD REFINED

Scripture Lesson: Deuteronomy 10:14–22

When, by the grace of God, I get to heaven, I would like some day to take Moses by the hand and lead him to Katharine Lee Bates. "Moses," I want to say, "meet Katharine Lee Bates. Miss Bates, meet Moses. You two have a great deal in common."

I'm sure they can find one another without my help, and may already have done so before I arrive. But it won't be the first time an unnecessary introduction has been made, and it would give me a great deal of pleasure. And if they care to take the time, of which there will be plenty in eternity, Moses and Miss Bates will then have an opportunity to commiserate with one another.

You see, they both tried to warn their respective nations about the dangers of success; national success, that is. And although their words are often repeated (in Miss Bates's case, sung), we still don't know the degree to which their counsel has been heeded.

Success is always hard to handle. Failure may number its victims in the thousands, but success numbers its in the ten thousands. That's because the perils of success are so subtle and so seductive. And if success is dangerous for an individual, it is even more dangerous for a nation. If we are at all sensitive as individuals, we know we should be ashamed of ourselves when we become carried away with our own success. But when it is the success of our nation, we sanctify it, so that instead of feeling some restraint, we are inclined rather to glory in the supposed achieving, and to cloak it in patriotism.

Moses had a problem on his hands—not at the moment he was speaking, but he knew it was coming. He could already feel it in the carriage and conduct of his people. As the book of Deuteronomy describes it, the nation of Israel was on the edge of the land of promise, the territory toward which they had set themselves some forty years before, when they escaped the slavery of Egypt. Moses was about to depart. Years before, he had done a stupid, sinful thing, and God had said that he would never be able to set foot himself in the promised land. But now, as his people awaited their grand entrance, Moses began delivering a series of warnings and advisements—the body of the Old Testament book of Deuteronomy, as we know it.

One of the things that especially worried Moses was success. His people were about to experience it, with a flourish. They were soon to have a land of their own—a land, he said, "flowing with milk and honey" (Deuteronomy 11:9). As a nation, they had been wanderers for forty years, and for more than four hundred years prior to that, they had been slaves. But now they were a full-scale nation, at least by the measure of the ancient world. Moses put the matter in dramatic terms: when your ancestors went down to Egypt, he said, they were just seventy persons; "and now the Lord your God has made you as numerous as the stars in heaven" (Deuteronomy 10:22).

So what do you do with success? Most of us revel in its power. And when you revel in power, you rarely use it well. Power is an awesome responsibility, not an ego trip. But of course, we don't easily see it that way. That's because success is a supreme intoxicant.

So Moses told his people what they should do with their power. But he did so in a roundabout way. He made his case like this: "For the Lord your God," he announced, "is God of gods and Lord of lords, the great God, mighty and awesome" (Deuteronomy 10:17). To put it in very human terms, Moses is telling them that God is a huge success, as big a success as can be imagined. So what is God doing with this success? See how Moses continues: the Lord God, he says, "is not partial and takes no bribe"; and especially, this is a God "who executes justice for the orphan and the widow, and who loves the strangers, providing them food and clothing" (Deuteronomy 10:18).

Isn't that astonishing? The God of the universe exercises power on behalf of those who don't have any power: orphans, widows, and aliens. Now, this is impressive enough however you read it, but all the more impressive if seen in the context of the world to which it was first spoken. For one thing, as Tom Cahill points out, the gods of the ancient world were always seen as being very susceptible to bribes; furthermore, they were prejudiced in favor of those who had, not of those who had not. And there was nothing about those popular gods and goddesses that was interested in justice; rather, if anything, they were interested in preference.

As for widows, orphans, and aliens, they were at the very bottom of the economic scale. They were the ultimate outsiders, without power, influence, or standing.

But Moses declares that God—this highly successful God— is concerned above all else with executing justice for the orphan and the widow. Still more unbelievable, God "loves the strangers," even to the point of "providing them food and clothing." What a remarkable God! Or perhaps you're thinking, how odd of God!

Now, if there is any preacher in you—or for that matter, simply any logician—you know what Moses is going to say next: "*You* shall also love the stranger" (Deuteronomy 10:19). That is, you ought to be like God. And then, if the appeal to godliness is not of itself persuasive enough, Moses adds a bit of a stinger: "for you were strangers in the land of Egypt" (Deuteronomy 10:19). If you aren't to be persuaded by an appeal to goodness and godliness, then be shamed into proper conduct by recalling from whence you've come.

But what does that have to do with Katharine Lee Bates, whom I'm so anxious to introduce to Moses? Perhaps some of you are even unsure as to who Miss Bates is, and why it is that I would take for granted that you'd be interested in her. Well, she was a graduate of Wellesley College who taught English there through all of her career. She wrote and edited a number of books in her field, none of which is likely to be available today.

But she had two remarkable experiences, as a result of which she has an everlasting place in American life. For one, she attended the Columbian Exposition in Chicago in 1893—a veritable "alabaster city" that was intended to symbolize the wonderful potential of America as it approached the twentieth century. Soon thereafter, she traveled across much of agricultural America, viewing the vast wheat fields; then, to Pike's Peak in Colorado, where she saw the majesty of America's great mountains. And out of it all, she wrote words that probably most of us will either sing or hear on this Fourth of July holiday:

> O beautiful for spacious skies,
> For amber waves of grain;
> For purple mountain majesties
> Above the fruited plain!

Now, if Miss Bates' poem had stopped there, we might still be singing it, but it wouldn't carry any nobility, and it wouldn't give me any reason to introduce her to Moses. The part of her poem that leaves me in awe is the refrain, when she becomes preacher, prophet, and woman of prayer. In each stanza, Katharine Bates moves from exulting in the wonders of America to a prayer for America. And her prayer has to do with her fear for America as it becomes a success.

I'm thinking particularly, at this moment, of these lines:

> America! America!
> May God thy gold refine,
> Till all success be nobleness,
> And every gain divine.

With remarkable human sensitivity, and with a conscience that would do credit to the Hebrew prophets and the Christian apostles, Miss Bates recognized that our gold needs refining. In its mined state, gold is generally crude; it's necessary to burn away the dross. Spiritually, the same rule applies. If wealth is not purified and consecrated, it becomes obnoxious in the extreme. It turns inward, making life ever smaller. It becomes ostentatious, so that its possessor looks ridiculous and doesn't know it. It affects the memory, so that one forgets his or her debt to others. And it corrupts the vision, until one cannot clearly see human need or human worth.

Apparently, Katharine Lee Bates saw those dangers clearly. Perhaps she recognized, as she looked at the alabaster city in Chicago's Columbian Exposition, that only a few miles away were unspeakable slums. And did she think, as she traveled through the wondrous "amber waves of grain," that its resources were often controlled by a few traders in the Stock Exchange?

As for the "purple mountain majesties," she had to know that there were those who would gladly rape and ravage those mountains if only they could get the coal, brass, or iron hidden in their bowels. No wonder she cried,

> America, America,
>   May God thy gold refine,
> Till all success be nobleness,
>   And every gain divine.

Well, we've made some impressive gains in roughly a century since Miss Bates wrote her words. A much larger percentage of people own their own homes. Life expectancy has been dramatically extended, and a college education is now more commonplace than was high school in Miss Bates's day. And of course, the vast majority of American homes now have indoor plumbing, electric power, refrigeration, and television. Yes, and a large number have computers and the Internet, too.

And yet, some statistics are very troubling. The gap between executive compensation and manual labor or factory labor is growing larger than ever—so large, in fact, that an executive who thinks he is that much better than his workers must have an ego that is larger, even, than his income. Has all success become nobleness, and every gain divine? Hardly! I fear there is no backstreet pornography that is more obscene than the figures that appear from time to time on the pages of our business sections.

I wonder what Katharine Lee Bates would tell us if she heard us singing her prayer on Independence Day. I think she might weep at how much we have, and—comparatively speaking—how little real *good* we're doing with it.

And what would Moses say? I think he might tell us that we are very impressive. Our economy is thundering along while the vaunted economies of other countries are faltering. But Moses will judge us by neither our gross national product nor our Dow Jones average. He will ask far more pertinent questions: How is it with the fatherless and the widow and the alien? How is it with those who have no political clout, who own nobody in Congress? Is there a voice of conscience in the halls of government, or in the church or synagogue? How many potential scientists, surgeons, clergy, artists, novelists, poets, and teachers are dying young in our slums, never getting even a glimpse of their own divine potential?

Moses would say, "See how *God* uses success: by caring for those for whom no one else cares. Be like God!" And Miss Bates would say:

> America, America,
> May God thy gold refine!
>   Till all success
>   Be nobleness,
>   And every gain
>   *Divine.*

Amen.

NOTES

1. Thomas Cahill, *The Gifts of the Jews* (New York: Nan A. Talese Doubleday, 1998), 154–55.

14

All Saints' Day

If the ancient church adapted some pagan holidays to its sacred purposes, our contemporary culture has gotten revenge with All Saints' Day—or, more particularly, the evening before All Saints' Day, known among us as Halloween. The takeover has been so complete that some Christians have consigned the whole package to the netherworld. They judge that Halloween is evil, at least as commonly celebrated, and extend the indictment to the day after, primarily by ignoring it.

That's a pity, because we need All Saints' Day. The church ought to do everything in its power to exalt and encourage sanctified living. Heaven knows, the other kind enjoys plenty of endorsements.

All Saints' Day is one of our oldest Christian celebrations. The church began honoring saints in its liturgy at least as early as the late second century and by the end of the fourth century had set aside a day for martyrs of the church. Sometime in the eighth century, the Catholic Church began using November 1 as the day to honor all the saints. That date continues to the present.

To measure the significance of the day in Christendom, consider this: in the British Isles, more than a thousand churches bear the name All Saints, a total surpassed only by churches named for the Virgin Mary.

There's a wonderful democracy in this holy day. Its purpose is to recognize all those saints who haven't been given a specific day in the church year. My years as a parish pastor have made me enthusiastic about such a celebration. I've never pastored a church, nor, for that matter, preached for a weekend in a church, without meeting some persons who seem to me to be true saints—and often with little recognition.

As the New Testament writers saw it, any of us who claim to follow Jesus Christ fall into the category of saints. Paul generously addressed his letters to the saints, even though many discussions in any given epistle would seem to make the title doubtful. No matter; we're made saints not by our merit but by God's grace. Perhaps more of us would come nearer the ideal if we took the possibility more seriously.

In many congregations, this Sunday includes some sort of memorial to those members who have died since the last All Saints' Day. In many instances, the church prints the names of these persons in its bulletin or Order of Worship, and perhaps reads the list as well. This practice has a kind of wholesome solemnity and it is often comforting and meaningful to family members, some of whom make a particular effort to be present. In other churches, this observance is part of the Sunday nearest Memorial Day. I would opt for All Saints' Day, to emphasize our Christian perception of death and memory rather than a more secular (even if very honorable) approach.

But let it be a great day for preaching. The lectionary will open many possibilities, and the occasion itself is rich with potential themes. And let there be a mood of glad celebration for the saints whose memory we honor, and high anticipation of our own calling to winsome holiness.

The sermon that follows was preached at Christ United Methodist Church in Memphis, Tennessee. When the church invited me to be the guest preacher, they noted that since it would be All Saints' Day, they would be including in the service of worship elements appropriate to the day. I sought in my sermon to take advantage of the setting and the calendar.

* * * *

A SPECIAL KIND OF GENIUS

Scripture Lesson: Philippians 3:4b–14

So today is All Saints' Day, and the bad news is that I have to persuade you that it matters. Roughly half of us care that Tuesday will be Election Day, and patriots care that Saturday will be Veterans' Day; and almost everyone (especially football fans and lovers of tradition and of food) cares that in a few weeks we will celebrate Thanksgiving Day. But All Saints' Day? With that news, the best I can get from most of us is a polite nod.

That's too bad, because if there's anything our postmodern world needs, it's some saints. Several of them. Several million, as a matter of fact.

Probably the biggest reason most of us aren't interested in saints is that we don't know what they are. We hear the word in church, and in some instances, we see likenesses in stained-glass windows. But saints aren't part of our daily conversation. They don't seem as important as another payment on the mortgage or getting an upgrade to our computer. Or, come to think of it, they don't seem as important as next week's football game. That's why we can slip through All Saints' Day without much thought.

So what is a saint? What if I were to tell you that a saint is a *genius*? Indeed, a very special kind of genius? This isn't my definition; I'm indebted to the late Phyllis McGinley, who won the Pulitzer Prize for poetry back in 1961. Some of you may remember her for her poetry in a variety of popular magazines, and for her autobiographical, humorous essays about being a wife in the suburbs, or her books for children.

For many years of her life, Miss McGinley, a devout Catholic, was fascinated by saints. She finally wrote a book about them. "What are saints," she said, "*except* geniuses—geniuses who bring to their works of virtue all the splendor, eccentricity, effort, and dedication that lesser talents bring to music or poetry or painting."[1]

Did you get that? Saints are geniuses who bring to their works of virtue all of these remarkable gifts that "lesser talents" bring to the fields where we generally look for geniuses. Now, if I had said that, you'd write me off as a preacher, with a preacher's prejudices. But Miss McGinley was a poet—a rather good one—and an accomplished writer; she was a praised and recognized talent. I venture that many of her friends did their thing in the world of music, painting, and the arts, and I'm sure she had a great deal of respect for their abilities. But she says that these esteemed accomplishments are for "lesser talents"! Nor is this a slip of the pen on Miss McGinley's part. In one way or another, she says the same thing again and again in her book. Virtue, she says, is our human "Everest, and those who climb highest are worth admiring."[2]

There was a man nearly twenty centuries ago who had the gifts to be a genius in several different fields. Literature? His letters are still read in hundreds of languages in every part of the world. His ode to love ("If I speak in the tongues of mortals and of angels"; 1 Corinthians 13) may be the most famous short essay to be found anywhere, on any subject. He was a genius in literature. But when I read his letters, I also realize that he had a genius for statecraft. If he had chosen to enter the political world, he might well have written a positive paper that would make Machiavelli be forgotten.

And let it be noted that he had the ambition and the heritage to bring his gifts as a genius to fulfillment. He lets us in on his story in our Scripture of the morning. I have "reason for confidence," he says (Philippians 3:4). And he did. He had a superb education, the first-century equivalent of Ivy League training. He came from good stock. His family had won distinction within their community. And like most geniuses, his talents demonstrated themselves early. While he was still a young man, no more than in his early twenties, he was elected into one of the most prestigious bodies in his culture.

But one day a tremendous change came into his life, and from that time on he turned all the power of his genius potential in one direction. And in the end he became a genius—the highest form of genius. He became a saint. We call him Saint Paul.

It occurs to me that some of you may not like Saint Paul. Specifically, you disagree with some things Saint Paul taught—or to be more correct, you disagree with some things that someone has told you he taught; it's quite possible you haven't checked the matter out for yourself. But of course, you don't have to like somebody to admit that the person is a genius. Bill Gates is a genius in the world of computers, but I know nothing about his personality. I'm enthralled by the genius of Thomas Wolfe, the early-twentieth-century novelist, but I don't find his life altogether admirable. So lay aside your personal feelings about Saint Paul for a while, and consider the genius that he became.

Recognize early that sainthood didn't come easily for Paul. His inclinations were not toward perfection. When you read his letters, you realize that he was sometimes given to self-pity. This is a very human trait, one to which we all succumb at times, but it isn't a very pretty trait. And sometimes he would boast. Not often; and when he did, he was ashamed of himself for doing so. Nevertheless, he gave in to boasting. And every now and then he was defensive. Sometimes I want to say to him, "Paul, get off it. We know who you are; stop being so defensive."

So I don't think it was easy for Paul to be a saint. But maybe it never is, for real saints. I think again of words from Phyllis McGinley. She was nearly convinced, she says, "that it is easier for a flamboyant sinner to achieve heaven than for an ordinary virtuous, complacent man."[3]

Perhaps we've unearthed a key issue with that little quote: *complacency*. I doubt that there are any complacent saints. Saints are always impatient with themselves and the state of their souls— not fretful, not self-despising, but driven to be better than they are. And yes, this is the measure: not that we should be better than our neighbors or our competitors but better than *we* are. This is our goal, and it is an unceasing and demanding one.

And that's what we see in Paul. He confesses that he hasn't yet reached his goal, but "straining forward to what lies ahead, I press on toward the goal for the prize of the heavenly call of God in Christ Jesus" (Philippians 3:13–14). This isn't a young Olympian writing. At this point Paul is in his fifties, and there's every reason to wonder if he will live out another year, because enemies are seeking his execution. But he hasn't settled into complacency. He is pressing toward the mark. He wants to be made perfect. Paul was content with life, but not with his level of goodness. He was happy, he said, with little or lots; it didn't really make any difference. But he was not content with who he was as a person. He wanted to be perfect in Christ.

Several years ago, as I completed a sermon at a church in Oregon, I invited anyone who wanted to be anointed for healing to come forward so the pastor and I might pray for them. I asked each one what he or she wanted from God: physical healing, burdens lifted, emotional healing, help in work. One of the first to come forward was an elderly man who had caught my eye through the whole service. His face had the beauty that is the mark of a saint, the kind of beauty that is the product of a long and perhaps painful process. When I asked him what he was seeking, he said, "I just want to love my Lord better." This is the mark of a saint. Saints are always striving for more purity of character, for more true godliness. The way an Olympic runner struggles to cut one-tenth of a second from her time, and the way an entrepreneurial genius seeks to add one more company to his corporate holdings—that's the way a saint seeks to drop one more distraction from the walk with God, and to add one more kindness to his or her thinking and doing.

But I suspect some are saying just now that they still can't see why being a saint is such a big deal. In a world where there are elections to be won, mortgages to be paid, conference championships to be had, and children to be raised, being a saint seems like a nice incidental accomplishment, but hardly a major issue.

Well, the fact is, it may be that the only reason the world is still holding together is because of its saints. We have to cope with so much of a downward, disintegrating pull, you know— on every side, and at every level. Whether we discuss international strife in the Middle East, the threat of war someday with Communist China, or simply the struggle for purity in the privacy of our own souls, the struggle is great, and the odds are sometimes frightening.

Consider the downward pull in our world. In business, it's the pull to cut corners; in politics, to be taken captive by every passing public opinion poll; in entertainment, to let our taste become cheap and coarse; in our minds, to let crude words, concepts, and images corrupt us. And much of the time, this downward pull is so subtle that we really don't know what's happening to us. What is to keep our world from slowly slipping into a quicksand of shoddiness that will someday make living unbearable? And what will keep our international community from one day blowing itself into oblivion?

Just one thing: *saints*. Jesus called such the "salt of the earth," the leaven that keeps the world buoyant. In the dark, hopeless streets where death and ugliness reign, a Mother Teresa walks. Christian laypeople go each week into prison compounds, to lead Bible studies and to listen to sometimes lonely, sometimes angry souls. Devout Catholics go each morning to their mass, and devout Protestants open their Bible each day, to read and pray. Such meaningless acts, some would say—nothing like the power brokering on Wall Street or the clever manipulating in the entertainment industry. Ha! While all of these are parading their power in New York, Washington, D.C., and Los Angeles, the saints are going to their morning prayers, where they hold back the very powers of hell.

Phyllis McGinley said that virtue is life's Everest. I would say that the pursuit of saintliness is life's ultimate decathlon. It is the most demanding enterprise in all of life's Olympics.

But let me add a special word. Saintliness is also the most democratic pursuit our world offers. Here is a realm of genius that is open to every human soul. Not many people have the literary genius to be a Shakespeare, the musical genius to be a Johann Sebastian Bach, or the athletic genius to be a Michael Jordan. But anyone—absolutely *anyone*—can become a saint.

Paul, probably in his fifties, said, "I don't have it yet." I, in my seventies, confess the obvious: I don't have it yet. But I know that it is the one thing in life absolutely worth pursuing. Because, as Paul said, this is why Christ Jesus made us his own—not simply that we might escape hell but that we might become like him; that is, that we might become part of that extraordinary community of the "strangest and highest form of genius," saints.

I haven't dared in this sermon to give you four simple rules for saintliness. To do so would be a kind of obscenity, because there's nothing simple about it. And in truth, it's a long journey. But it is a wonderful, magnificent journey, and I can't think of a better day on which to begin it than today: All Saints' Sunday! A perfect time to begin approaching the ultimate Everest. A perfect day to set out to be a genius.

NOTES

1. Phyllis McGinley, *Saint Watching* (New York: The Viking Press, 1969), 18.
2. Ibid., 4.
3. Ibid., 65.

15

Thanksgiving Day

I like Thanksgiving Day! By definition, it is a civil holiday, rather than a religious one, and yet its roots in our biblical tradition are older than most of our stated religious occasions. Celebrated rightly, the mood of the day seems to me to be the mood that ought to characterize every day, every moment. I preached on the thanksgiving theme on the Sunday preceding Thanksgiving each of the sixteen years of my pastorate at the Church of the Saviour in Cleveland, Ohio, and at a few union Thanksgiving services as well, and always found it easy to come upon a new approach, a new metaphor, a new reason for celebrating the day. This is a tribute not to my creativity but to the wonder of the topic.

The particulars of the American Thanksgiving holiday are generally well known, though one does well to check out details in an encyclopedia before including them in a sermon; inaccuracy in small things can diminish one's believability in weightier matters. Most references to the Thanksgiving story seem to center on the Pilgrims and on Presidents Washington and Lincoln, and with good reason. But we would do well to remember Sarah Josepha Hale, who, as editor of *Godey's Lady's Book*, led a campaign that may have been crucial in establishing Thanksgiving as a national holiday. (Incidentally, Ms. Hale also gave us "Mary Had a Little Lamb.") We probably owe a debt, too, to England's harvest-home celebration, which no doubt influenced the settlers at both Jamestown and Plymouth in their development of a thanksgiving festival.

We preachers will want to remember that this holiday has biblical roots in the harvest festivals of Israel. This witness should not be lost in the community celebration of the holiday. Thanksgiving Eve is now one of the most visible ecumenical occasions in the average community. What once was a union Protestant service is now, in many places, a service involving not only Catholic, Eastern Orthodox, and Jewish bodies but also one or more of the Eastern religions. The Christian clergy will seek to avoid offense but will nevertheless remember the sacred roots of our Thanksgiving celebration. Any ecumenical celebration that diminishes a faith, including one's own, defeats the very essence of ecumenism.

A Thanksgiving sermon should never be too deeply philosophical, though certainly it should have a base in the Scriptures. But it is never detached from life. It ought, like the Psalms, to name names, places, and events. Thanksgiving is remembrance. It isn't necessarily positive in all its reports, because a proper sense of thanksgiving sees life with faith, so it recognizes that sometimes gratitude begins with "nevertheless." And because the sermon relates to real life and real events, it will often have personal elements. I dared once to preach a Thanksgiving sermon that was almost strictly a personal testimony. I did it carefully—indeed, cautiously—but it was well received, perhaps partly because I had been pastor long enough for my people to receive such a personal witness, and partly because I dealt with the data in such a way that the congregation could relate to the stories and see how much they were like their own.

A special admonition: don't try to *convince* people to be thankful. Gratitude is something to which we're converted, not something of which we've been persuaded. You know as much from some family or friendship occasion where someone speaks of someone or something for which they're grateful, and soon others are chiming in. There's something communal about gratitude. Let a single, gentle voice be heard, and before long there will be a chorus. You'll feel this in people's hearts as you preach, and some of your listeners will tell you so after the service.

I preached this sermon for a chapel service at Union College, Barbourville, in the Kentucky mountains. You will see references in the sermon that identify the location and the academic way of life.

* * * *

ALL DRESSED UP IN HAND-ME-DOWNS

Scripture Lessons:
Psalm 105:1–9; Matthew 6:25–34

The nicest suit I had during my teenage years was a hand-me-down. It happened during the great economic depression of the 1930s. Like one-fourth of the population at that time, my father was in and out of work, and even the work he had was marginal, so we managed with the barest necessities. My mother never lost her middle-class tastes and outlook, however, so while we ate like the poor people we were, mother insisted that I must somehow have a Sunday suit, one I could also wear for the two or three big events of the school year.

Unfortunately, any suit we could afford to buy didn't do much for me. We would have been glad to accept some hand-me-downs, but people my size were rare in those days. I was six feet, four inches tall and weighed 154 pounds, so I wasn't likely to inherit clothes from anyone; and for the same reason, bargain-counter suits simply didn't come in my dimensions.

Then, one summer day, my cousin Winston stopped for a visit. He was perhaps fifteen years older than I, and he was a high school teacher somewhere out west. In our working-class world, high school teachers were people you saw only in the classroom, not in your living room or on the front porch. I thought he was terribly glamorous, especially when he talked casually and familiarly about his fellow teachers.

Suddenly he paused and asked how tall I was. "Wonderful!" he said. "I have a suit I've grown out of. I'm too stout for it now. It should fit you almost perfectly. I want you to have it."

It was by far the best piece of clothing I had ever seen. My mother—a pretty able seamstress—altered it only slightly to make it fit. I'll never forget the first Sunday I wore it to church—part of me fearing someone would ask where I got it, while another part feared my friends would think I had become superior by wearing something so clearly out of my class. But by the second Sunday, I wore it with grace—with as much grace, at least, as my ungainly frame wore anything. It might be a hand-me-down, but now it was *mine*, and it fit. My cousin Winston may have bought it, but now it was mine.

As the years have gone by, I've become comfortable wearing hand-me-downs. Most of my possessions are in that category. Not my clothing; I buy my shirts and suits and ties firsthand. But nearly everything else I have has been passed on to me by someone else, and I'm glad and grateful.

That's the very essence, for instance, of being in an educational institution, whether it's kindergarten, college, or graduate school. We're here to put on some hand-me-downs. They're exquisite! Many of them are classic lines. Speak of Euclid in geometry, Pascal in mathematics, Aristotle in philosophy, or Shakespeare in literature, and you're talking of garments that have been around for a very long time, and with quality to die for. Wear them with pride.

And wear them with humility, too, acknowledging that they *are*, indeed, hand-me-downs. Don't worry about altering the wisdom of the ages so it will fit you. If we will submit ourselves to the kind of scholarly discipline that will take off some of our intellectual flab and fat, we'll be surprised at how good we look in the garments of other ages.

But education is only a small part of the hand-me-downs we wear. Mind you, it's a strategically important part, especially for those of us on a college campus. But it's still only a small part of the story.

Take buildings, for example. I've studied in scores of public and institutional libraries, and I never built or bought or paid rent on one of them. I've had the privilege, counting summer terms, of study on half a dozen or more campuses, and in every case it was a hand-me-down. The buildings were there before I came, and I couldn't have paid the rent for a day, let alone a term. So, too, with art museums: even when they've charged admission, I've known I was there mostly by charity.

Or consider medical care. We pay for it, of course, and pay rather substantially. But the knowledge that treats us is something that's been handed down not only since Hippocrates but also from the Hebrew Scriptures in the book of Leviticus. Medical science has advance to a degree that would have been inconceivable even twenty years ago, but it's all built on gifts from the past. Any medical care you and I receive is an accumulation from centuries of benefactors.

By now I think you know what I'm driving at. I'm doing nothing other than calling us to celebrate Thanksgiving. It's time to look at our intellectual, social, political, economic, and spiritual wardrobe and give thanks for all those "cousins" who have blessed us with hand-me-downs. This family to which you and I belong, this human race, is sometimes a pain and an embarrassment. But never forget what a wardrobe of good they've passed to us. Thanks be to God for the millions of cousins who've blessed us by passing along the benefits of the centuries.

The biblical writers understood this. They respected their heritage. When the people of Israel spoke of their faith, they often identified themselves as worshiping the God of "Abraham, Isaac, and Jacob." This was the way they confessed that they were indebted to their ancestors for the faith that held them. They had the humility and the intelligence to recognize that they lived in the midst of what had been given to them, passed on down.

They not only recognized it; they found strength in it. So it is that a great Old Testament poet rejoiced in

> the covenant that [God] made with Abraham,
>   his sworn promise to Isaac,
> which he confirmed it to Jacob as a statute,
>   to Israel as an everlasting covenant.
>   (Psalm 105:9–10)

Call it name-dropping if you will. When the uncircumcised world around them pointed to their own graven images and challenged the Jews for their religious artifacts, the Jews gladly answered that their faith had been handed down to them— from Abraham, Isaac, and Jacob; from Moses and Miriam, Deborah and Barak. The Psalms, in particular, are full of the names and events of the past, to remind the people that they are the blessed beneficiaries of generations of faith, and of the unceasing goodness of God.

It's a poor human being who doesn't want to footnote his or her life this way. If we can tell our life's story as if it were all our own doing, we're fools or knaves or a blend of the two. Begin the story with a simple sentence, "I was born," then insert the scholar's arabic 1 and enter the footnote "I owe this to my mother and father." Continue with the sentence "From the outset, I had dreams and aspirations," then enter your arabic 2 and put in the footnote "I owe this to God, who made me an eternal creature, full of grand expectations." And so it will go through all of your story, until the footnoting will reach three digits within a single chapter, and you know you must begin the next chapter with arabic 1; otherwise, the numbering of your footnotes will become astronomical.

Machiavelli is not usually considered one of the more admirable characters of human thought, even though he has left us with a seminal document, "The Prince." But he was wise enough to be humble. During a period when he was in semiexile, and his daytime hours were spent in laborious tedium, he looked forward to his evenings. He would then quite purposely dress himself in courtly garments for his time of reading. Why such dressing up? Because, he said, he was going to "enter into the courts of ancient men, where, being lovingly received," he would feed on that food for which he was born. Thus, for four hours each evening, he would "give [himself] completely over to the ancients." Machiavelli not only knew that he had been blessed with hand-me-downs; he considered these hand-me-downs such an honor that he must dress with dignity to receive them.

But I've touched only the outer fringes of life when I speak of these matters that have come primarily from our human family. Above all, each moment and until the end of life, in more ways than we can ever imagine, we receive hand-me-downs from the Lord God of the universe. Jesus put it elegantly: "Consider the lilies of the field," he said, "how they grow; they neither toil nor spin, yet I tell you, even Solomon in all his glory was not clothed like one of these" (Matthew 6:28 29). Tune in some day to that portion of the weekend news that includes a fashion report, watch the models stride disdainfully in the latest designer creations, then say to yourself, "Any field flower can do better!" And the flowers are there, in abundance—sometimes in the nurtured lines of a garden but sometimes in a parking lot, where they've pushed their way through asphalt.

God sends these favors with reckless generosity. I look out each morning on the mountains that encompass our area [Barbourville, Kentucky] and acknowledge gratefully that they contain more strength and grandeur than I can ever take in. My heart beats something like a hundred thousand times a day, and I give it not a thought unless for some vagrant reason it skips a beat, or if some staircase accelerates its action. I rub shampoo into my scalp and take for granted the computer that is housed by that scalp—a computer that performs so many functions of such variety that you and I will never plumb a fraction of its potential.

So what did we do to deserve all this beauty and power and wonder? Not a thing. They were handed down to us at birth, and—like the grace of God—are made new to us every morning. What have we done to pay for them? Not a great deal more, comparatively speaking, than the lilies of the field have done to pay for the loveliness the Creator has invested in them.

Especially, and above all else, I am blessed by communion with God—indeed, even to the point of salvation. A good woman in one of the cities where I preached earlier this fall said to me, "I'd like to say that I'm a Christian, but that sounds as if I'm boasting." If being a Christian were an achievement, it would indeed be boasting to claim it. The standard is so high that only a person of little self-insight would dare to think he had deserved it. But being a Christian is not an achievement; it is a gift. It is ours not by an interminable process of human effort but by the grace of one who said, "Let anyone who wishes take the water of life as a gift" (Revelation 22:17). It is another of the gifts handed to us by an unbelievably kindly God; the greatest gift of all, because of the quality of eternity that it brings into this life, and the promise of eternity that it offers beyond this life.

So I sing the song, this Thanksgiving week, of someone who is all dressed up in hand-me-downs. In a sense, I suppose it's humbling to acknowledge the source of my wardrobe. But on the other hand, there's a satisfaction in the wearing if I've come to the place where the garments fit, and fit so well that they look as if they were always intended for me. And it's satisfying, too, if I live in such a way that I'm contributing to the hand-me-downs that others will someday wear.

But most of all, I realize that the hand-me-downs I have been given are luxurious beyond compare, and that there is almost no end to what might still be added to my physical, intellectual, social, cultural, and spiritual wardrobe. So why should I be embarrassed to be dressed as I am, particularly since everyone on this planet gets his or her wardrobe in the same shop? Instead, I will simply say *thank you*: to history, to friends and family, to books and culture, and, most of all, to God. Thank you, for getting me all decked out in these magnificent, incomparable hand-me-downs!

16

Christmas

Parish pastors approach their Christmas preaching task in quite different ways. Many avoid any pure Christmas theme in either music or sermons until Christmas Day, emphasizing instead the Advent theme. This approach is supported by centuries of tradition, although I think it must be said that it is better understood by clergy and by church musicians than by the average person in the pew. Others begin using Christmas music and carols soon after Thanksgiving and preach rather broadly to Advent, Christmas, or general themes until the Sunday before Christmas or Christmas Eve, when they opt for a full-scale Christmas emphasis.

I have no desire to shape or reshape anyone else's Christmas preaching. In my own pastoral days, I almost always preached an Advent series (four sermons) and surprised myself by the variety of possibilities I found for such a plan. I think my sermons might sometimes have been judged inappropriate by an Advent purist, but I hope that on the whole I met the needs of my people.

In any event, I'm very sure the preacher should take full advantage of this season. Who, in any field, sacred or secular, gets as much free promotion and advertising as does the preacher in the Christmas season? I can choose, if I want, to complain about the secularization of Christmas, and surely such a complaint is justified. I choose instead to adapt the outlook of the legendary Cecil B. DeMille—something to the effect of "I don't care what you say about me as long as you mention my name." For the weeks of Christmas shopping and celebrating, "the name" is being mentioned; it's up to us to redeem the scene and make the most of the common interest.

The Protestant pastor will broaden his or her preaching by some research into the practices of Catholic and Orthodox bodies, and also by examining the traditions of various ethnic groups. Go beyond seeing the quaint to understand the depths from which the presumed quaintness comes.

The preacher and the church musicians should be a team at all seasons, but especially during Advent and Christmas. And both preachers and musicians should have proper empathy for matters of sentiment. Christmas is a sentimental season. This can make for superficiality and for some very hazy theology, but it can also provide a setting in which superb truths are better heard. Don't exploit sentiment, and don't be afraid of it; make it an honorable ally.

The sermon that follows was preached at the Park United Methodist Church in Lexington, Kentucky—a rather small neighborhood church, with a good share of older persons but a representation of young families and of college and seminary students. The pastor, a very effective homiletician, was preaching a series on the words of Christmas. When he asked me to be part of the series, I chose a word he hadn't included: *fear*.

* * * *

BE AFRAID!

Scripture Lesson: Matthew 2:1–8, 16–18

Before I go further, I had better level with you. This morning I feel pretty much like Ebenezer Scrooge before his change of heart, or like the Grinch who stole Christmas. Here we are, at the season of songs, parties, and general goodwill, and I step into the pulpit to say, "Be afraid!" It's as if everyone is singing in lovely harmony, like a scene from Currier and Ives, and I'm off at the edge, beating a cymbal off key and out of time. Who wants to be told, at such a lovely time as this, "Be afraid"?

Of course, with a little thought most of us will remember that fear is a recurring part of the Christmas story, but it always turns out well. When the angel Gabriel came to the Virgin Mary, Mary was frightened, but the angel said, "Do not be afraid" (Luke 1:30). When Joseph was worried about the future, an angel told him, "Don't be afraid to take Mary as your wife" (Matthew 1:20). And when, on a hill outside Bethlehem, an angel appeared to a little group of shepherds, the shepherds were terrified. But the angel told them not to be afraid, because he was bringing them good news (Luke 2:10).

But I'm reporting on a different scene. I want to tell you about someone in the Christmas story who was afraid, and who had good reason for such a feeling. No angel told him, "Fear not." If an angel *had* come, the angel would have said something like "You have plenty of reason to be afraid, and you'd better do something about it."

Let me tell you the story. Much of it is familiar to you, but perhaps not at the parts I want to emphasize. Sometime not long after Jesus was born, some wise men came to Jerusalem looking for him. These wise men were a peculiar breed; it's hard to categorize them for our twenty-first-century world. Perhaps they taught in some university, or perhaps they belonged to some sort of ancient think tank. They were true scholars, and our rather pretentious times should remember as much. Nowadays, a scholar is likely to be a specialist in a very limited field; as a matter of fact, with the explosion of knowledge, the

fields become more limited and confining every day. These
first-century wise men were students of mathematics, astron-
omy, logic, and philosophy. And the particular wise men in our
story were also, I'm confident, passionate seekers after truth.

In the midst of their research and their seeking, they came
to believe that a baby was to be born who was to be the king of
the Jews. They believed it because they had seen a star in the
east that they concluded was portentous. Now, you and I can
easily write off this idea as some astrological superstition, but I
think there was more to it than that. Of course, every generation has its superstitions. Probably some future generation will
be amused by our fascination with public opinion polls. And I
wonder what they will say about literary deconstruction or
about our handling of history. So I don't like to be too conde-
scending about the intellectual fads and superstitions of other
generations.

I suspect that when these wise men came to believe that a
king of the Jews had been born, their conviction was partly a
result of their studies of history, of literature, and perhaps of the
Hebrew prophets, as well as their study of the stars. However
it was and whatever it was, these men were so deeply convinced
that they engaged in a long and arduous journey in order to find
the baby king.

Many of us get ideas that move us enough to make us say,
"You know, somebody ought to do something about that." At
other times we're so moved that we make a contribution. But
very rarely are we so moved that we invest a sizable sum of
money and a large piece of our time, perhaps even to the point
of forsaking our other responsibilities. Obviously, these wise
men were profoundly moved—moved to the point of expensive
and perhaps even perilous action.

When the wise men got to Jerusalem, they found a kind of
dead end. They couldn't locate the baby or anyone who knew
anything about a new king. The capital is the place a king
should be found, but no one in Jerusalem had such an idea. If
anything, I think the wise men found people avoiding their
questions, looking over their shoulders to see who might be lis-
tening before venturing even the most innocuous answers.

But soon they had an audience with King Herod. Herod had heard about these wise men. He had followed through with his own research and had learned from the chief priests and the scribes that according to the prophet Micah, the someday-king would be born in Bethlehem. Herod wanted to know what the wise men knew, so he called them in for a secret conference. And he did so, the Gospel writer Matthew tells us, because he was *frightened*: "When King Herod heard this, he was frightened, and all Jerusalem with him" (Matthew 2:3).

Now, in many ways, King Herod was not very bright. He was a terribly cruel man, and one can't be so cruel and also be truly intelligent, because cruelty is in its own way a lapse of rational thinking. But I'll tell you this: Herod was intelligent enough to be frightened. He knew his throne was in danger.

You see, Herod was a very insecure man. Interesting, isn't it, that someone can be king yet be insecure? But of course history is full of such instances, and so are our daily papers. Whether today's Herod is a president, a corporate executive, an entertainer, or a champion athlete, he or she can still be insecure. There's no achievement, no diploma to be hung on the wall, no record set that can give one a sense of security. Security goes deeper down than that. And Herod didn't have it.

In truth, Herod is an enigma—as all of us are, in some measure or other. On the one hand, Herod was a very effective ruler. He brought peace and order in Palestine, and that wasn't easy to do. He built the temple in Jerusalem that is usually referred to as Herod's Temple. He was sometimes admirably generous; he remitted taxes to help the people, and during the famine of 25 B.C.E., he melted his own gold plate to buy food for the poor. But as William Barclay has pointed out, he was "almost insanely suspicious," a quality that seemed to grow with age. Anyone he saw as being a threat to his throne was simply eliminated. To be specific, he murdered his wife, Mariamne, and her mother, Alexandra; his oldest son, Antipater; and two other sons, Alexander and Aristobulus.[1]

When you recite that record, you agree that Barclay was right in describing Herod's suspicious nature as almost insane. And you understand what follows in the biblical story. Herod may have been insane, but he was also crafty. As I mentioned earlier, he called in the wise men, talked with them about their research so he could get as much data as possible about the time of the baby's birth, then sent them on to Bethlehem with the request that when they found the child, they bring word back to Herod so that he could "go and pay him homage." Of course he intended no such thing. Perhaps you will recall that after the wise men found Jesus, they were warned in a dream not to return to Herod. This brought Herod's mad fears to an even higher level of terror, so that he ordered the execution of all the children in and around Bethlehem who were two years of age or younger. But by that time, Jesus was gone.

So Herod was afraid—insanely afraid. But he was right. If you're a king, and you want to remain king, Jesus Christ is the ultimate threat. And I'm struck by the way the Bible tells the story; it reports that Herod was frightened, but that "all Jerusalem [was frightened] with him." I don't think the writer was referring to the general populace; I venture the man on the street never heard the matter. But those who ruled Jerusalem, who along with Herod had a stake in the throne, were frightened—as frightened as Herod was. Even a tyrant has those around him who know their security rests in the tyrant's continuing in power. So, like Herod, they were afraid.

Jesus doesn't really seem such a threat, of course. He surely didn't in Herod's day, nor does he today. It's nothing less than amusing that Herod was frightened by the rumor that a baby was putting his throne in peril. Herod had the power of Rome at his disposal—soldiers, money, political affiliations. What could an unknown baby do to such power as that? But Herod was afraid. Call Herod an insecure fool, a megalomaniac frightened by his own shadow—no matter. Herod was right. Herod didn't know what he was up against, but he was right in being afraid. This was the most profoundly lucid moment of Herod's life. The conduct that followed was abominable, of course, but the fear was wise.

And so shall it ever be. Just over four hundred years ago, Robert Southwell, a Jesuit priest, pondered the power of the infant of Bethlehem and wrote,

> This little Babe so few days old,
> Is come to rifle Satan's fold;
> All hell doth at his presence quake,
> Though he himself for cold doth shake.[2]

Southwell died a martyr at only thirty-four or thirty-five years of age, but he knew the power of the tiny babe of Bethlehem— power enough to make him willing to suffer martyrdom! Herod was against the babe and was frightened; Southwell was for the babe, and he was unafraid.

It's popular today to say that we have entered the post-Christian era; that is, our Western culture has now become almost entirely secular, and Christianity is no longer an issue. If one watches television for an evening, one would have to say that our world is, indeed, post-Christian. If our age has any gods, they must be money, sex, sports, automobiles, running shoes, and a variety of toys for all ages. How much is Jesus Christ an issue, unless one tunes in to a specifically religious program?

But it's probably little different from the world into which Jesus was born. On that ancient night, the people of Bethlehem were wondering how to pay their taxes, and the people in Jerusalem and Rome were discussing political questions, and the literati in Athens and Alexandria were pondering the latest wrinkle in philosophy or poetry. They didn't know that away in a manger a baby had come to "rifle Satan's fold." So I would suggest to Washington and Wall Street, to Broadway and Hollywood, to Las Vegas and Atlantic City, to Paris and Hong Kong, London and Singapore: Get as smart as Herod. Quake in your Guccis, because a King has been born, and ultimately, he will win.

But Herod is not my big issue, nor is Wall Street or Washington. The crucial issue for me is the person I supposedly know best, the one who lives in my chest and selects my necktie every morning. I remember a sociology class half a century ago. The professor was talking about personality types. There are those, he said, who must be called the "king type," because they want to be boss; they want to run things. The young woman sitting next to me (whom I hardly knew) leaned over and said, "That's your type."

Now, I could complain that she was brash and unduly free in sharing her opinions. But as it happens, she was also right. That *is* the kind of person I am. And forgive me for mentioning it, but that's you, too. We're all people who want to be king or queen. Some of us don't get a very large throne, but we make the most of it. We start with our crib, from which we scream out our orders, and we generally keep at it, as much as society and good taste will allow, until we're on our deathbed. We like being king or queen.

So when word comes that a King has been born in Bethlehem, we ought to be as frightened as Herod. Because the day is coming when every knee will bow to this "helpless" baby (that's what the Bible says), and every tongue will confess that he is Lord. It would seem wise to recognize him now, while time and circumstances are on our side.

Here, then, is a Christmas word for you and for me: Be afraid. If your name is Herod (and everyone's name is), then be afraid. Because the King has come, and he is going to win. This little babe, in swaddling clothes, is going to win. Brothers and sisters, boys and girls, it is time to get off the throne, and to give the throne to the only one who is eternally qualified to reign. Amen and amen.

NOTES

1. William Barclay, *The Gospel of Matthew* (Philadelphia: Westminster Press, 1958), 1:19–20.
2. Robert Southwell, "New Heaven, New War," in *The Roads from Bethelehem*, ed. Pegram Johnson III and Edna M. Troiano (Louisville, Ky.: Westminster/John Knox Press, 1993), 117.